Your PhD Guide

Accessible, insightful and a must-have toolkit for all final year doctoral students, the founders of the 'Thesis Boot Camp' intensive writing programme show how to survive and thrive through the challenging final year of writing and submitting a thesis.

Drawing on an understanding of the intellectual, professional, practical and personal elements of the doctorate to help readers gain insight into what it means to finish a PhD and how to get there, this book covers the common challenges and ways to resolve them. It includes advice on:

- Project management skills to plan, track, iterate and report on the complex task of bringing a multi-year research project to a successful close.
- Personal effectiveness and self-care to support students to thrive in body, mind and relationships, including challenging supervisor relationships.
- The successful 'generative' writing processes which get writers into the zone and producing thousands of words; and then provides the skills to structure and polish those words to publishable quality.
- What it means to survive a PhD and consider multiple possible futures.

Written for students in all disciplines, and relevant to university systems around the world, this unique book expertly guides students through the final 6–12 months of the thesis.

Katherine Firth manages the academic programs of a residential college at the University of Melbourne, Australia and founded the Research Insiders Blog which has been running since 2013.

Liam Connell has worked in research training and education since the late 2000s. He works in research development at La Trobe University, Australia.

Peta Freestone has worked in higher education for over 15 years, creating award-winning initiatives including Thesis Boot Camp, founded in 2012. She designs and delivers writing and productivity programmes for universities and other organisations around the world.

Insider Guides to Success in Academia
Series Editors:
Helen Kara,
Independent Researcher, UK and
Pat Thomson,
The University of Nottingham, UK

The *Insiders' Guides to Success in Academia* address topics too small for a full-length book on their own, but too big to cover in a single chapter or article. These topics have often been the stuff of discussions on social media, or of questions in our workshops. We designed this series to answer these questions in to provide practical support for doctoral and early career researchers. It is geared to concerns that many people experience. Readers will find these books to be companions who provide advice and help to make sense of everyday life in the contemporary university.
We have therefore:

(1) invited scholars with deep and specific expertise to write. Our writers use their research and professional experience to provide well-grounded strategies to particular situations.
(2) asked writers to collaborate. Most of the books are produced by writers who live in different countries, or work in different disciplines, or both. While it is difficult for any book to cover all the diverse contexts in which potential readers live and work, the different perspectives and contexts of writers goes some way to address this problem.

We understand that the use of the term 'academia' might be read as meaning the university, but we take a broader view. Pat does indeed work in a university, but spent a long time working outside of one. Helen is an independent researcher and sometimes works with universities. Both of us understand academic – or scholarly – work as now being conducted in a range of sites, from museums and the public sector to industry research and development laboratories. Academic work is also often undertaken by networks which bring together scholars in various locations. All of our writers understand that this is the case, and use the term 'academic' in this wider sense.

These books are pocket sized so that they can be carried around and visited again and again. Most of the books have a mix of examples, stories and exercises as well as explanation and advice. They are written in a collegial tone, and from a position of care as well as knowledge.

Together with our writers, we hope that each book in the series can make a positive contribution to the work and life of readers, so that you too can become insiders in scholarship.

Helen Kara, PhD FAcSS,
independent researcher
https://helenkara.com/
@DrHelenKara (Twitter/Insta)

Pat Thomson PhD PSM FAcSS FRSA
Professor of Education, The University of Nottingham
https://patthomson.net
@ThomsonPat

Books in the Series:

Publishing from your Doctoral Research
Create and Use a Publication Strategy
Janet Salmons and Helen Kara

'Making it' as a Contract Researcher
A Pragmatic Look at Precarious Work
Nerida Spina, Jess Harris, Simon Bailey and Mhorag Goff

Being Well in Academia
A Practical Companion
Petra Boynton

Reframing and Rethinking Collaboration in Higher Education and Beyond
A Practical Guide for Doctoral Students and Early Career Researchers
Narelle Lemon and Janet Salmons

The Thesis by Publication in the Social Sciences and Humanities
Putting the Pieces Together
Lynn P. Nygaard and Kristin Solli

Your PhD Survival Guide
Planning, Writing, and Succeeding in Your Final Year
Katherine Firth, Liam Connell, and Peta Freestone

Your PhD Survival Guide

Planning, Writing, and Succeeding in Your Final Year

Katherine Firth,
Liam Connell, and
Peta Freestone

LONDON AND NEW YORK

First published 2021
by Routledge
2 Park Square, Milton Park, Abingdon, Oxon OX14 4RN

and by Routledge
52 Vanderbilt Avenue, New York, NY 10017

Routledge is an imprint of the Taylor & Francis Group, an informa business

© 2021 Katherine Firth, Liam Connell, and Peta Freestone

The right of Katherine Firth, Liam Connell, and Peta Freestone to be identified as authors of this work has been asserted by them in accordance with sections 77 and 78 of the Copyright, Designs and Patents Act 1988.

All rights reserved. No part of this book may be reprinted or reproduced or utilised in any form or by any electronic, mechanical, or other means, now known or hereafter invented, including photocopying and recording, or in any information storage or retrieval system, without permission in writing from the publishers.

Trademark notice: Product or corporate names may be trademarks or registered trademarks, and are used only for identification and explanation without intent to infringe.

British Library Cataloguing-in-Publication Data
A catalogue record for this book is available from the British Library

Library of Congress Cataloging-in-Publication Data
A catalog record has been requested for this book

ISBN: 978-0-367-36183-9 (hbk)
ISBN: 978-0-367-36184-6 (pbk)
ISBN: 978-0-429-34439-8 (ebk)

Typeset in Helvetica
by River Editorial Ltd, Devon, UK

Katherine, Liam and Peta would like to dedicate this book to all the PhD students who have told us their stories, shared their experiences, asked us questions and given us feedback on our advice.

We'd also like to dedicate this book to over eight years of teamwork. We did finally write it all down.

Contents

List of illustrations   xiii
List of abbreviations   xiv
Acknowledgements   xv
About the authors   xvi

Introduction   1

PART I
Focusing on the project   9

1 Defining the project: What is my thesis for?   11

2 Getting through the crunch   20

3 Practical project management   28

4 Working with your strengths and weaknesses   47

PART II
Focusing on the person   57

5 'No pain, no gain' and other unhelpful myths   59

6 Your harshest critic   72

7 Getting unstuck 86

8 Working with your supervisor 90

PART III
Focusing on the text **107**

9 Getting words down 111

10 Making the thesis into a coherent work 128

11 Making the words good 162

PART IV
Finishing the PhD **177**

12 Reflecting on what it means to be a researcher 179

13 Do you actually want to finish the PhD? 183

14 Relief and grief of finishing a PhD 191

Index 199

Illustrations

Figures

9.1	Katherine's Writing Cycle (see Mewburn, Firth and Lehmann 2019)	112

Tables

3.1	Progress on Goals to Complete the PhD	30
3.2	Using the Pomodoro Technique	40
4.1	Keeping a research journal	53

Abbreviations

IMRAD	Introduction, Methods, Results, and Discussion thesis structure
OED	Oxford English Dictionary
PhD	Doctor of Philosophy degree
QILT	Quality Indicators in Learning and Teaching (Australia)
SMART	Specific, Measurable, Achievable, Realistic, Time-bound goals
SUAW	Shut Up and Write
TAC	Transport Accident Commission
TBC	Thesis Boot Camp

Acknowledgements

The authors would like to thank the series editors of the *Insider Guides to Success in Academia*, Pat Thomson and Helen Kara, for their swift, professional and warm shepherding of this manuscript through to completion.

We would like to thank the three beta-readers, themselves in the final stages of the PhD, who generously took time to carefully and thoughtfully engage with the text and made a number of suggestions that made the work much better and more useful.

Thank you to Sarah Tuckwell, our editor at Routledge, and to Lisa Font and Rebecca Collazo, and everyone else in the editorial and production teams without whom this book would not exist.

About the authors

Dr Katherine Firth is the author of a number of books about academic writing, including How to Fix Your Academic Writing Trouble with Inger Mewburn and Shaun Lehmann. Her blog Research Degree Insiders has been running since 2013. She is also a published poet, translator, and literary scholar. She currently manages the academic programs of a residential college at the University of Melbourne.

Dr Liam Connell has worked in research training and education since the late 2000s, designing and developing curriculum and pedagogical tools for PhD candidates across ethical leadership, interdisciplinary project management, research design, academic identity, and how teams collectively solve problems that can't be answered by individuals working alone. He currently works in research development at La Trobe University, Australia

Dr Peta Freestone has worked in higher education for over 15 years, creating award-winning initiatives including Thesis Boot Camp. Currently, she designs and delivers writing and project management programmes for universities and other organisations around the world. When not teaching, she writes fiction. Her novels have been published in eight languages.

Introduction

You can survive, and thrive

'So, when are you going to finish your PhD?' is a question often asked by well-meaning family, friends, or non-academic colleagues. For some PhD students, it's a question that can be answered as neutrally as talking about the weather. But for many more, it can feel intrusive and shame-inducing. It doesn't matter if you are finding the PhD harder, longer, or slower than you hoped. You can survive, and thrive, even through the challenging final year of writing towards submitting your completed thesis. And that's what we want for anyone who has just picked up this book.

What this book is about

This book focuses on the final 6–12 months of completing a PhD. Katherine, Liam, and Peta realised that we were having the same conversations with people at a similar point of the PhD, over and over again. We knew there was a wealth of useful and insightful literature published about how to start a PhD, including how to plan a methodology, build a literature review, establish good research habits, and develop a working relationship with a supervisor. Confusingly, these books were often called things like How to Finish Your PhD. But there was comparatively less material focused on how to navigate those sometimes messy, often difficult final months.

We acknowledge that there is a broad variety of experiences that grow out of a PhD student's individual journey to get to the point where they are a year or less from finishing. The paths that people take to being post-thesis are just as diverse. Students have a range of academic backgrounds, personal circumstances, and strengths. Therefore, we offer here the most common advice and strategies that we deliver in workshops. Don't worry if you don't conform exactly to our suggestions or guidelines – you can still succeed. Just pick out the tools that seem most relevant to your circumstances.

Why we wrote the book

One of the seeds from which this book germinated was our collective work on an intensive writing programme that specifically helps research students finish their thesis: Thesis Boot Camp (TBC). In some ways, this project has become 'Thesis Boot Camp in a book'. But it is still important to talk about how the Thesis Boot Camp programme can go beyond what's offered in these pages.

Peta was the original designer of the award-winning Thesis Boot Camp, drawing from research and from models in the USA, and her own experience (the irony is not lost on her) of struggling through the late stages of her PhD. Doctoral-specific writing support has long been offered in the United States (Lai 2014; Link 2018). But after conducting an online review and consulting with universities such as Princeton, Stanford, and Marquette, Peta identified a gap in graduate writing support and developed a new programme that built on international best practice to bring in new aspects of student support.

TBC is a carefully structured programme. It's based on extensive research into factors leading to successful writing, and on our years of experience in academic development and student support. It helps doctoral students to:

- Achieve significant progress on their thesis draft,
- Finish their PhD faster and with less stress,
- Master strategies for effective writing that will benefit their future career.

TBC helps universities to:

- Increase the rate of timely completions among doctoral cohorts,
- Provide a powerful intervention that prevents late-stage attrition,
- Improve the student experience, earn goodwill and boost graduate satisfaction.

TBC was developed specifically for late stage students who have read, thought and processed for years before they attend. The intensive 'camp' itself takes place over three days where students are set a 'stretch target' of 20,000 words. It supports participants by providing them with the tools, time, space, motivation, and confidence to make serious progress on their thesis draft, and maintain momentum. It is designed to help participants acknowledge the practical, intellectual, social, and emotional issues that impact the final stages of their doctoral journey, and put strategies in place to address them.

We are all big believers in experiential learning. The best way for participants to understand that they truly can produce a large volume of academic writing in a limited timeframe, is to have an experience of that and see the outcome for themselves. As Greg Dening wrote 'we never learn the truth by being told it. We need to experience it in some way' (1996, 316). We'd agree.

That's why TBC has two key intended outcomes. The first is that students leave with new material for their thesis that they can begin to refine afterwards. The second is that they have had a different experience of academic writing, without having to take the risk of trying the strategies on their own.

If you have a Thesis Boot Camp available at your campus, we encourage you to participate. If there isn't one currently available, further information is available on how to bring Thesis Boot Camp to your campus at thesisbootcamp.com. Since 2014, we have been working in partnership with universities around the world to introduce the programme to new cohorts. The evidence – both anecdotal and systematically collected – clearly demonstrates that the programme empowers people to continue when they may have otherwise dropped out, and helps them complete in less time and with less heartache. We've seen first-hand how Thesis Boot Camp transforms lives.

How to use the book

We see this book as a 'survival basics' guide. We think there is a real use for a slim volume that covers the basics of the final year of a PhD – because we often talk to students who haven't been given the information, support, or training they need. Meanwhile, if you're reaching your milestones satisfactorily, people might assume you're 'on track' and know exactly what to do without them telling you. We know you are smart and able to do independent research. But you can't know what you don't know! So, this book can give you a jumping off point to find more information that is specific to your exact circumstances, or to tweak our strategies to work best for you.

You can read the whole book early on to get a quick overview of the likely challenges you'll face in the final stages of the thesis, along with the tools to tackle those challenges. You might call it the 'pack ahead' approach. Supervisors who want to be prepared to support their students in the final year might also find the book helpful for an overview of potential advice they might offer.

But you can also use this book in an emergency, quickly consulting it in the middle of deadline stress, supervisor conflicts, or when your writing has stalled or ground to a complete halt. You should be able to find a tool, pull it out and use it immediately to help you keep moving. Because every part of the PhD is linked up, we often had a debate about the best place to discuss particular tools, but we'll always refer you across to sections with other relevant tools. We also recommend using the index to construct your individual tool kit.

Because it's a 'survival basics' book, we keep our advice at quite a high level. We recognise that your individual contexts will vary significantly: your family circumstances, work commitments, language of instruction, personal health, and social network all impact on your experience of the PhD. So we encourage you to use our advice as a basis for developing tools and techniques that work for you.

The shape of a doctoral thesis or a doctoral degree can be radically different even within a single university, so we encourage you to also find specific regulations, advice and examples that are directly relevant to your degree. We also know that the language used to speak about doctoral degrees is fundamentally different around the world. Please mentally replace 'PhD' with whatever you call your doctoral degree; 'supervisor' with whatever you call the principal academic(s) responsible for guiding your studies; 'thesis' with whatever you call the long, written research document; 'chapter' with the articles or other component parts of your thesis; and 'student' with whatever people who work towards a research higher degree are called where you are. The principles will be the same, even though the language may change.

The structure of the book

This book is divided into four parts, each one addresses a major component of the final year of the PhD.

Part I is all about the PhD as a **project**, and you as the project manager steering it toward completion. We look at clarifying your core arguments, understanding your thesis' purpose, getting through the final crunch period, harnessing your individual strengths and identifying potential weaknesses. Along the way, we offer practical project management strategies.

Part II is focused on you, the **person**, the one who actually has the big responsibility of bringing the degree to completion. This part of the book is about *person*-management. We look at a range of unhelpful myths about the PhD which might be causing you unnecessary stress, strategies to beat back mindsets that might be getting in your way, and dealing with supervisory relationships that may have become difficult.

Part III is dedicated to the thesis as a **text**. We explore how to regularly get words down onto the page with the least amount of stress, plus how you can turn all of those disparate ideas into a coherent, cohesive work that is alive with your scholarly voice, and ready for examination.

Finally, Part IV is about being **finished** with the PhD, whether that's submitting a thesis or deciding that it's right for you to quit. We have a look at the things that are great about being finally done with a PhD, and we also tackle the less-than-great aspects. We include these challenging topics because we believe knowledge is empowering.

Taken together, these four parts reflect our 'PhD philosophy': that it is a **project**, which will be completed by a **person**, ideally in a healthy supported environment. This person will submit an original academic **text** developed through a range of academic conventions. And when **finished**, you will not just contribute to a scholarly field, but will have changed who you are as a researcher and thinker.

References

Dening, Greg. 1996. *Performances*. Chicago: University of Chicago Press.

Lai, Paul. 2014. "Academic guides: residencies & capstone intensives: PhD residencies." Walden University Writing Centre. https://academicguides.waldenu.edu/writingcenter/residencies/phd.

Link, Stephanie. 2018. "Scaling up graduate writing workshops: From needs assessment to teaching practices." *Journal of Writing Research* 10, no. 2: 357–399. doi:10.17239/jowr-2018.10.02.07

Part I
Focusing on the project

A PhD is a complex project, one that requires working with various stakeholders, managing time and tasks, communicating effectively, meeting deadlines and solving problems. While project management skills are important throughout your PhD, the final year has some unique challenges. New skills to meet these challenges will be needed whether you have been adding to your document for years, have a portfolio of work or publications, or are just now sitting down to write up.

This part of the book first helps you to define your project scope and find ways to articulate your contribution to your field. Next, we'll look at how and why the end of a project is often called the 'crunch'. The crunch is intense. It's nothing like the early or middle stages of a project, and it's rarely discussed in books that give advice about PhDs. We'll therefore provide practical techniques to save you time, help you stay focused, and reward you when you make progress. These are the skills we have all transferred to our jobs managing projects, and then transferred back to writing projects like this book, so we know they work.

You will also have to come to terms with the ways in which the PhD won't be perfect, something that is true for every project. Nonetheless, the PhD, and you as a researcher, will have unique strengths, and so we finish this first part of the book with advice on how to identify those strengths.

1 Defining the project
What is my thesis for?

The argument

What actually is a thesis? You might not feel entirely comfortable asking this question with less than a year to completion, but it is worth being clear.

You may have heard supervisors tell you over the years that you **have to have an argument**. You might have given a chapter draft to someone in your department to look at over a weekend, and then have that moment – perhaps over coffee, first thing on a Monday morning – when they put their cup down with a *clink* and look you in the eye and say, 'but what's your argument?' We often ask students this question ourselves, in one-to-one coaching sessions. We frequently get a response like:

> I dunno, I just … know what I'm interested in, I know what I want to find out, where I have to go to find it, and I reckon I have the skills to do that. Who am I supposed to be arguing with?

The students we speak to often have a lot to say about their topic, especially after researching it intensively for years. And yet, that doesn't always translate into an argument as understood in academic writing.

A 'thesis' is usually defined as a foundational idea or theory that can be advanced with evidence. The root of the word is Greek, meaning 'to place something' or 'to put something forth' (OED online 2020). It is a contention at the heart of a longer discussion (or dissertation) that will elaborate the justification for that contention.

A thesis is, literally, an academic argument. It is a position you take on a question or a problem that has yet to be resolved. In its broadest terms, that is all it is. The document you end up submitting is therefore an argument that is sustained over the course of its length, comprised of supporting parts, usually chapters, each of which contributes something to making and sustaining that argument.

A typical challenge is being able to precisely articulate exactly what this argument is. Most thesis-writers know deep-down what they are trying to say, but can't yet do this in a crisp, clear, concise way. If that sounds like you, how should you go about identifying or explaining your argument? This advice is for people who pretty much know what their argument is, but haven't necessarily clearly articulated it yet. If you are earlier in the process, we suggest other in-depth resources (e.g. Chapters 3–6, Thomson and Kamler 2013; Chapters 4 and 7; Kamler and Thomson 2014).

Questions and scoping

It's good to start by succinctly articulating your top-level research question. Sometimes when we ask people about

Defining the project 13

their thesis question, they give us a paragraph-length reply, or they tell us, 'well, I actually have three research questions. The first one is …'. That's fine, all those questions are likely valid queries that deserve your attention. In some fields of study, six research questions are normal. But even then, there will be the question or the problem or the issue that sits above them all. What is the issue that binds them all together?

Sometimes when we ask people what their central research question is, we get an instant rapid-fire response. These thesis writers have been pushed to articulate it before: they've practised it, they've wrestled with it, and it is now as familiar as a limb. And if that's you, you should have no trouble articulating it in one sentence.

Others have never had to really confront this before, and the process of doing so is hard work. But it is absolutely worth doing. A useful overall thesis question is usually a single sentence long. So, as a thought experiment, if you had to summarise in one sentence what the central question that your project-as-a-whole will attempt to answer, what would you write?

This question may not be formally written down in your thesis anywhere, but even so, have a go at writing that question out. What is the thing that we don't know enough about, that your project will address, and that each chapter will unpack in a lot more detail and nuance?

You might use one of these prompts to help you formulate or re-formulate your question.

- *How is …*
- *Why are …*
- *What is …*

14 *Focusing on the project*

- *What should …*
- *What could …*

Think about the question. Put the book down and write it out now.

> The central question that my entire thesis seeks to answer is:

This is your **thesis question**, and we want you to be really clear about it.

An effective thesis question should require a response that can be demonstrated with evidence, but that can still invite debate. Briefly, it should not be too simple, narrow, vague, descriptive, or without internal coherence.

Here are some examples of how to make your thesis question more effective:

- Too simple: *When were hamsters introduced to North America?*
  Better: *What were the chief drivers of hamster population growth in North America in the nineteenth century?*
- Too narrow: *At what rate does the efficiency of cutting through grass blades correlate with hamster-teeth sharpness?*
  Better: *How have changes to bone structure from crossbreeding affected hamster nutrition and lifespan?*
- Too vague: *Why do parents buy hamsters for their children?*
  Better: *What effects on social development of children does owning hamsters as pets have?*

- Too descriptive: *What happens to their fur when hamsters moult?*
  Better: *What are the evolutionary benefits of seasonal fur moulting to hamsters?*
- Without internal coherence: *Have hamsters been affected by climate change and if so are the effects larger than in guinea pigs?*
  Better: *What are the causal links between hamster reproduction rates and climate change?*

If you look at your overall research question and it appears to fall into one of these traps, it is likely that you need to adjust your **scope**, either to make your argument more analytical, manageable, sophisticated, or allow you to 'open up' your discussion.

Clarifying and crystallising your core research question allows you to sharply define the limits of your study – what is **in scope** and what is **out of scope**. It can be tricky because you need to make binding decisions about what you're researching and why, particularly when you're approaching a complete first draft of the work.

Making decisions about scope can be painful. You might have conducted a significant body of research that you decide is no longer going to be part of your thesis because you've realised you need to reduce your scope. If that's you, then you are going to cut a lot of material out of your thesis that you have laboured over. This is difficult, but your thesis will ultimately be the stronger for it. And, remember, whatever is removed can often be repurposed for a separate journal article or conference paper.

Perhaps after reading this far, you feel you could have a second, improved, go at writing down your central thesis question. We are definitely believers in multiple drafts, so here is another chance to refine:

> The central question that my entire thesis tries to answer is:

Answer statements

When you have your **thesis question** written down and in a form that feels right, the next challenge is to ask yourself: what is my **answer** to that question? If you had to summarise your answer in one sentence, what would that sentence be? Again, it is just a thought experiment. The sentence itself may not actually turn up anywhere in your thesis.

Have a look again at your thesis question that you wrote out earlier. Based on everything you have researched, and all the data you have gathered, and everything you have read, and everyone you've spoken to – even if it all changes next week, but at *this* moment – what is your answer to that question, in a single sentence? Unlike the thesis question, if you want to expand your single sentence into a paragraph, then go right ahead.

This sentence is your **answer statement**. You might sometimes see this described as your 'position', or 'view'. The answer statement contains the essence of your overall argument for your thesis. When someone says to you, 'so what's your argument?', they are asking you to tell them your evidence-based response to your overall, central research question. What is the position that you are taking on the core question or problem that your thesis will address?

Defining the project 17

Now, of course that answer statement is a very high-level summary of what your argument is and will be. The fullness of what you will contribute to your discipline through your thesis will always be vastly more nuanced and complex than this one-sentence answer. Each of your chapters will unpack that detail and contribute a piece to the reader's understanding of your argument. Nevertheless, it is worth keeping a version of this high-level answer statement in your mind. It is the thing that you learned from your research that you want the world to know.

If you are in the final year before you submit your thesis, now is the time to articulate your thesis question and answer statement. Now is the time to go from thinking about the work as a chapter-by-chapter proposition ('what is this chapter about?', 'what is the next chapter about?') to thinking about your entire project as a whole coherent entity. We want you to be articulating these things now, today, especially if no one has pushed you to define these things before.

Spending an hour refining and clarifying your thesis question and answer statement will repay you in many ways. The benefit of writing it out now is that it will help clarify your thinking. Step back from the detail in the separate chapters, give yourself space to consider the big picture and put it into words, even if those words are for your eyes only. It will sharpen your understanding of your research and provide something tangible to seek feedback on, to further refine as you head towards completion. Does the statement make sense to your supervisors? If so, how? If not, why? If your core idea is too vague or nebulous, or is bogged down in detail, it will not be so easy to explain.

You are the only person who knows the answer to your thesis question, so make sure you can explain it to yourself, your supervisors, and your examiners. Your supervisors might have said to you on a few occasions, 'it's *your* thesis'. That's because examiners want to know where you are in the contribution you are making to your discipline. Examiners want to see that you have a strong grasp of the literature, that your research design is sound, that you have a critical eye for the evidence, that your methodology is useful, and your findings meaningful and robust. Most importantly, they want to be told what it is that *you* are saying about the question you are researching: what your evidence tells us that we did not know before, and why we should care about it.

The first full draft

We want you to articulate your core argument right now so you are ready to work towards a complete first draft of your thesis. A complete first draft of the whole project, no matter how rough, is a critically important milestone in your journey as a PhD student, second only to actually finishing and delivering the entire work.

Our experience is that when you have a complete first draft of the whole thesis, you are around 85% finished. Until the first draft is finished, it often seems easier to stop and quit than to push on. When you have a full first draft, we argue, you reach a mental and intellectual tipping point whereby it becomes **easier to continue than to stop**.

This is the moment when your whole thesis goes from being an idea in your head or in disparate fragments, to an actual artefact in the world. You can see the overall shape. It has a beginning, middle and end. No matter how much refinement is needed, the document exists. From here on in, it's not about whether you have enough things to say, it's about the words you choose to tell the story of your research.

At this point, you want to be transitioning away from thinking chapter-by-chapter to thinking of your project as a whole. That is why we want you to be thinking hard, now, about what your overall research question is, and what your answer to that question is. Your **thesis question** and **answer statement** become the critical lens through which you will view that first full draft. They will also drive editorial decisions about what stays in, what is deleted or becomes a separate publication, and most importantly what are the areas that need to be fleshed out or improved so that they more effectively serve your central argument, to move your thesis closer to submission.

References

Kamler, Barbara and Pat Thomson. 2014. *Helping Doctoral Students Write: Pedagogies for Supervison*. 2nd ed. Abingdon: Routledge.

OED Online. March 2020. "thesis, n.". Oxford University Press. www.oed.com/view/Entry/200655

Thomson, Pat and Barbara Kamler. 2013. *Writing for Peer Reviewed Journals: Strategies for Getting Published*. Abingdon: Routledge.

2 Getting through the crunch

The final stage of a major project is often referred to as the 'crunch' time, a critical period of high intensity just before the deadline. In a PhD crunch, you may also be trying to carry off several 'firsts' simultaneously: the first piece of original research you have designed, conducted, and reported on; the first time you have had to manage a project of this scale and complexity; the first time you have taken the role of project lead and are responsible for drawing all the parts together to bring the project to completion.

It can all become overwhelming. You might be asking yourself where all the time and space to explore concepts and research plans have disappeared to. It might feel like you don't have time to spend on anything but work, and even then you won't make it. However, to help you through, we'll shine a light on what the 'crunch' stage actually is for PhD students. We'll then give you practical time and task management strategies to help (but also see the time management techniques specifically for writing in Chapter 9).

Possibilities vs. constraints

A crunch period is a standard feature of just about any project. Building an IT network, trialling new vaccines,

Getting through the crunch 21

building a skyscraper, producing a film – all of these projects have a final period during which people furiously wish they had 'just a bit more time', and 'just a bit more money' to finalise their project the way they envisioned it. There is not a project manager alive who has not, at some point, wished for more time and resources in the final stages of a project.

Why does this happen? Because large projects that evolve, change shape and go on for years and years, always discover unexpected problems that they couldn't have anticipated. This is probably what is happening with your PhD, and probably it *should* happen. If you started a PhD, mapped out your 3.5 years of hypothesis, literature review, data collection, results analysis, discussion, conclusion, completion ... and the project went exactly that way, all smooth sailing, then we would be asking two questions. One: if it was so straightforward, have you actually discovered anything new? And, two: did you learn anything from facing challenging situations that you can apply elsewhere? A PhD is more likely to be a convoluted process: where you have to think creatively about how to achieve your goals, against the clock and with limited funding, while you struggle towards the breakthrough – the *aha* moment – and then work out how to communicate that new understanding to other people.

Another reason why the crunch period is difficult, is that you, as the project lead, have to make binding decisions about what goes in your thesis, and what stays out (as we said in 'Questions and scoping' in Chapter 1). Earlier in the PhD, you will have been casting your net wide, collecting as much data as possible, keeping your options open about what your argument is and what areas your research will actually cover. Now, during the project crunch, you have to decide with cold-eyed clarity what is feasible to do in the time remaining, and what material, though interesting and possibly a joy to engage with, has to be jettisoned. It's hard because you might find all the material you collected fascinating, you might be acutely aware that it is original, that no one else has dealt with it or thought about it the way you have. We're sorry, but too bad. If it does not help support your core argument, it has to go. If it does not help your reader understand what that core argument is, it also has to go. And sometimes it is just a matter of budget mathematics – doing that extra piece of interesting work is likely not in the time budget (we'll look at making a 'writing time budget' in Chapter 3).

Think about your experience of research being on a graph, with the horizontal axis being months in the PhD and the vertical axis being all the ideas and research concepts that you can usefully engage with and use in the thesis. The first six months of the thesis should see a large uptick in that graph: you can do anything, and every week exposes you to new concepts you would love to include in your thesis. The last six months should see the reverse, you narrow in, reduce your scope, focus sharply on what is *necessary* and *possible* within the time and resources available to get the thesis finished. Your new mantra becomes: 'this is interesting, but not for now'.

Will it pass?

You're in the project crunch phase right now. And like every other project manager, you have to be realistic about what time you have left, and just get it over the line. Finish it. By hook or by crook, complete the job. This book is full of advice and strategies about how to make that journey from where you are now to when you submit your thesis for examination, but the core advice is to *get it done*. The only way out is through.

A key point to remember is that while your thesis will be examined closely, it will not be graded like a coursework dissertation. There are no A's or Firsts or Distinctions for a thesis. Ultimately it will pass, or it may fail. If it passes, it might pass without any further work needed, or it might pass with some revisions required. In a tiny minority of cases, it could fail. Your thesis just has to pass. It is not possible to submit an A+ or H1 thesis.

Of course, you have poured so much effort in over the years and want your thesis to be as strong as it can possibly be. But always remember your thesis just has to pass. When considering the scope of your thesis and looking at the list of tasks needed to complete the work, the question to ask yourself, 'if I change or reduce the scope in *this* way, is the thesis still cohesive and coherent, and also, *will it still pass?*' If the answer is yes to both, then consider it seriously as an option.

Use the 'will it pass?' question when seeking feedback on your chapters. When you give your supervisor chapters to review, you are naturally going to want to know their feedback at the deeper conceptual level. You will be asking them to tell you things like: 'Does it make sense?' 'Is the argument convincing?' 'Does the evidence support the argument?' But you should also be asking, 'Will it pass?' If the answer is 'no', then ask them what you need to do *precisely* in order that it will pass.

If you're struggling with getting the feedback you need, see Chapter 8 for advice on communicating with your supervisor. Good academics will critique and provide feedback on problems with your argument, evidence or theory all day long. We are trained to always challenge ourselves to get better. But reframing the conversation by asking them, 'But will it pass?' will help you put their feedback in perspective. Is your work looking good with the potential to be endlessly just a little bit better, or are there serious issues that will stop you from passing?

Going fast, but not moving

See if any of this sounds familiar:

Monday morning, bright and early, you are on your way to work. You're thinking about all the stuff you have to do today. There is a conference next month, but you haven't started on the presentation. You want to make progress on a chapter draft that has been hanging around for months, and if time allows, prep for a class you need to teach on Wednesday.

Ok, that chapter has been bugging you for ages. You decide it'll be the first thing you tackle today.

At your desk, you open your laptop ... and see a bunch of emails that came in over the weekend. The conference organisers sent out a reminder that your paper is due by the end of this week. And some of your students emailed on Sunday to ask questions about an assignment. So first you go through and deal with your inbox.

Getting through the crunch 25

Then your door opens and your office buddy comes in. As he boots up his computer, you have a quick chat, partly about work, but partly about the weekend. You both settle down to get to work. Except it's already time for a meeting with your supervisor.

She is a great supervisor who always makes time for her students, and the meeting turns into lunch. She will be heading off on travel later in the month, and she'd like to have a draft of that thesis chapter from you before she gets back. It should be done by now, but the data collection was trickier than anticipated. You tell her it shouldn't be too far away.

After lunch, you *must* get this conference paper started to meet the deadline. You write half a page. But then you worry that you have you haven't prepared for your Wednesday class. You'd better switch tasks.

At 4:30 p.m., you remember that your thesis is the *actual* reason you're here doing any of this other stuff at all. You open your files and realise you'd really like to have a look at the data first, to refresh your memory about the specifics of your findings. You discover you haven't finished analysing it yet and you can't start writing (so you think) until you do that.

Ping! Your email goes off again and it's your co-author for the conference paper. She has made a start on the PowerPoint. Great! You send a reply. Now you notice your stomach is growling, so quickly go and have something to eat, and come back to the office.

It's quiet now, just after 7 p.m. Finally! A chance to get some work done. But what? You haven't finished the teaching prep, the conference paper is due at the end of the week, that data analysis is still not working, and you haven't written a word of your thesis. You feel frustrated and nervous and exhausted.

Why? Let's look at what you wanted to get done today:

- Make a start on the chapter draft that's been hanging around for months.
- Draft your half of the conference paper for Friday.
- Prepare for a class on Wednesday.

And what did you actually get done?

- Answered student emails.
- Met with your supervisor.
- Talked to your office buddy.
- Did a tiny bit of data analysis.
- Did a minor amount of preparation for Wednesday's class.
- Wrote half a page of the conference paper.
- Wrote zero actual words of that thesis chapter.

You were busy, you are exhausted, but it feels like you have nothing much to show for the day. You spent long hours at work, can honestly say you were not slacking off, yet somehow you've got through almost none of the things that you wanted to. As you go to sleep that night you ask yourself, how did it happen? Worse, how did it happen *again*? With variations on the specifics, today looked like a lot of other days last week, and the week before that, and the one before that too.

In the above scenario the student had quite a few advantages: they have limited teaching responsibilities and they are able to spend ten hours in the office on campus if they want to. If you have an outside job, caring responsibilities, a long commute, a disability that impacts your studies, or don't have a dedicated study space ... You may only be able to sit down to your thesis sporadically or for much shorter periods of time. Still, you'll probably recognise the feelings in the scenario, whether you face external challenges or internal ones. We know what going faster but not moving feels like. We have done research alongside other jobs, or while dealing with long-term health issues or challenging situations at home. So, let's give you some practical strategies.

3 Practical project management

Seeing your PhD as a project gives you the chance to learn project management tools and techniques, or to use skills you might have built up from employment. We think the most critical skills for the final stage of the PhD are realistic goal setting, consistent progress tracking, and disciplined time management. We focus on the techniques and tools that we recommend most frequently, and that we successfully use ourselves.

Goal setting

While your overall goal is to complete your PhD, that will be achieved through a combination of smaller goals, which in turn are made up of big and small tasks. (If you aren't sure if your overall goal even *is* to complete, skip forward to Chapter 13 'Do you actually want to finish the PhD?')

First up, you need to work out what your goals are. Lots of people will tell you what your goals ought to be. However, it is much more effective if you make goals that align with your personal goal-setting and goal-achieving styles. You also should set goals that are realistic for you.

Once you have set your goals, you should be clear how you will judge if you have met your goal. Measuring your goals may be achieved by something quantitative like meeting a word count, or it may be something qualitative like 'my supervisors and I agree it's finished'.

As you are in the later stages of the project, you probably aren't starting from zero on many of these goals. So, check how much progress you have already made, and then work out how much is left to be done. This stage can feel a bit scary, but most people are surprised by how much they have achieved already.

There are lots of ways to map your goals towards completion, and we will describe some of our favourite tracking techniques later in this chapter. Whichever tracking technique you use, you need to define the parameters.

Your goals to complete the PhD might look something like those in Table 3.1.

It sounds straightforward. But beware: we have all set goals that didn't help us. Setting the wrong kind of goal for you personally often means you're planning for failure.

Have you missed a deadline recently? Obviously, you didn't consciously set yourself up to miss your target. It may be instead that you have developed unhelpful goal-setting habits. For example, the desire for a sense of achievement or control from completing projects sooner rather than on-time; wanting to impress or placate others; or not accurately factoring in all the variables. Perhaps you're an 'all-or nothing' type, where if one part of the goal slips, you give up on the rest, defeated. Perhaps you have habits that used to work but now are ineffectual.

Table 3.1 Progress on Goals to Complete the PhD

Task	Criterion for completion	*How much work left to get there?*
Clarify final version of thesis question and answer statement	(See 'Questions and scoping' and 'Answer statements' in Chapter 1)	
Finish a 'first full draft'	(See 'The first full draft' in Chapter 1)	
Complete any final research	(See Part IV 'Finishing the PhD')	
Structural editing	(See 'Structural editing' in Chapter 11)	
Copy editing	(See 'Style editing' in Chapter 11)	
Add your own		

Your style might have been developed in a context with very different demands from the late stage of a PhD, like your undergraduate years.

Do any of these resonate with you? Recognising your goal-setting style can be a powerful first step to escaping a cycle of missed deadlines. A reassessment can then give you the clarity you need to set more effective goals in the future.

Setting effective goals is more than just setting targets that fit a SMART (specific, measurable, achievable, realistic, time-bound) goals template, or any similar version. SMART goals don't work for every kind of task. What's more, many academics find them uninspiring, so they don't set them in the first place.

Be aware, too, that goals that are **simple to achieve** and goals that are **easy to achieve** are not the same thing. For example, you may have the goal of running a marathon within the next two years, when you've only ever run for 10 km. That is a simple, clearly defined and measurable goal with well-defined steps to achieve. Millions of other people have done it before you ... but that does not mean it will be easy to achieve!

It is therefore also important to remain mindful that your goals are realistic for you as an individual, with your particular learning needs, your project or academic discipline, and your life commitments outside of your PhD. If you thought you had set effective goals but you still didn't regularly achieve them, try reviewing the last three months as a diagnostic process. Use some of the 'tracking your progress' tools below to collect and analyse data to find out what you did that worked and where you could develop. What were the goals you set? Did you meet them? Where did you find it difficult or impossible? What happened there? And importantly, what can you do differently from here?

Tracking your progress

Have you ever set a big thesis writing resolution at the start of the academic or calendar year? Around these times, you've no doubt seen and heard friends, PhD peers and even academics declaring their writing output ambitions. Social media is abuzz with motivational hashtags. Water cooler conversations sparkle with a 'this time will be different' brand of hope. You think to yourself that 'this will be the semester I make serious headway on my thesis'. You may have gone as far as to identify the chapters you'll write. Or maybe you've challenged yourself to get to the end of the first draft.

As we said, goal setting is useful. But let's take a moment to consider a very real possibility: not achieving your goal.

Grand writing goals often fail because they rely on sustaining effort across a significant period of time, but the initial burst of enthusiasm languishes much sooner. Life starts to get in the way. And then the deadline you set rolls around and you look back, bewildered as to where all that time and motivation went.

Tracking progress is a simple yet powerful tool. By checking in with yourself daily or weekly, you'll stand a much higher chance of achieving longer term goals. You'll be able to address issues while they're manageable, rather than when they're spiralling out of control. Importantly, recording your progress can also help you understand what you can feasibly achieve in an hour or a day, which will make you able to plan your progress more effectively and better prevent deadline stress (Freestone 2018). (For more on deadline stress, see 'Myth 5: Deadlines are always motivating' in Chapter 5.)

Monitoring your output can also be a huge motivational boost. Rather than relying on the lure of the one big goal of completing your thesis, you get a more regular sense of achievement when you can say: 'I drafted 5,000 words this week!' or 'I edited ten pages today!' It helps you build or restore your confidence. If you feel like you're not making any headway, you can look back at the irrefutable evidence that things truly are moving forward. That alone can reconfigure your thesis writing goals into more carrot, less stick.

For example, Peta kept a Gantt chart in an Excel spreadsheet during her PhD. A Gantt chart is a visual representation of tasks and time in a project (for academic writing examples, see Pacheco-Vega 2018). Peta tracked the number of words written on each chapter in her thesis, and how much it contributed to the overall word count. When she hit the 50% mark, it felt like she had got through the hardest part of the thesis, and it became a much more exciting and less intimidating project.

If you Google time management tools, you will realise there are a daunting number of different approaches, and that everyone customises them to fit their own situation. All of these progress tracking techniques have one thing in common – they make the invisible, and seemingly insurmountable, work of finishing a PhD into something you can see. It is a much smaller cognitive load to check out your app or wall planner than to try to keep it all in your head. You can also show your progress to other people, like your supervisor or writing buddy. Finally, each of these techniques has a deeply geeky reward built in, whether you are motivated by data, tiny stamps, or stacks of writing journals.

To make the most of your time, you need to know **how you're spending your time**. The exact method you choose is completely up to you, but do decide on a method and use it consistently and regularly. You'll stay motivated and keep on top of your writing goals. We all still use our favourite PhD time tracking tools to write reports, journal articles and books like this one, so it's an investment in your future productivity too.

Setting your pace

'Pacemakers' or 'countdown tickers' are digital applications that help you keep things moving along in the desired or optimum rhythm. Enter in your goal and deadline, and then use the program to help you set your pattern and track your progress against your targets. Back when Katherine was finishing her PhD she had to hack a pregnancy countdown meter, but there are now lots of quite sophisticated trackers out there. Peta's Excel Gantt chart was basically a manual tracker. Don't just use them for word counts, you can use them for drafting, editing, proofreading and more. These days there's also tracking for exercise and other healthy habits.

Project management software often includes trackers for how much (or little) time you have left to complete a project to help you calculate how long a project will take to complete at a certain rate of progress, or tell you how much you need to accomplish each day to meet a time-bound goal. Software with this functionality for writers includes Pacemaker and Scrivener. These programs also help you tailor your efforts to your schedule. If Mondays are always full of meetings, then you won't be getting any writing done that day, and restrictions like these can be factored into what you need to achieve for the rest of the week.

If you're the sort of person who finds data motivating or reassuring, then make sure your tracker can give you graphs and tables that show you an overview of your progress. We won't lie – there's a certain thrill in seeing lines and numbers climb towards your overall goal each time you sit down and work on your thesis.

Plus, you can often share your tracker projects for accountability: another powerful way to help you stay on target.

Another crucially important aspect of a tracker is that if you do fall behind, you can get an idea of how you can catch up, or if you're going to have to renegotiate a deadline. It also allows you to compare how you've done in previous drafts so you can make realistic goals based on real data.

Sticker method: Not enthused by numbers and graphs? Try the Sticker Method to visually keep track of your writing progress. Don't make the mistake of thinking stickers are only for children – some of the most prolific authors writing today use this method to track their progress.

What's involved? Take one wall calendar or wall planner and acquire some stickers or stamps of your choice. Possibilities include stars, cute animals or sparkly rhinestones – just make sure they're fairly small in size. Decide on your units of measurement (100 words, 500 words, pages edited), and then add one or more stickers or stamps to each day on the calendar on which you achieve that goal.

You'll very quickly get a sense of how you're tracking by how colourful your calendar becomes. At a glance, you'll see productivity streaks and gaps, which can give you a better sense of your progress over time.

Writing journal: Are you a person who responds better to words than graphs or stickers? Try keeping a writing journal to track your progress. Your writing journal is a place to record your word output, alongside anything else relevant about your writing day.

Writing journals can be online or offline, but many people find a pen-and-paper journal is most effective. An easy format is to jot down your word count against each day in a standard diary, adding notes each week or month to review how you're tracking against your goals. From the simplest notebook to specialist all-the-bells-and-whistles productivity journals, there are many options. Be aware of the potential trap in exploring endlessly to find your perfect stationery, though. While the ready-made structure and the aesthetic appeal of productivity journals will suit some, there's nothing stopping you from getting yourself a plain notebook and applying the same principles.

Create a writing time budget

If you've been regularly missing writing deadlines, consider creating a writing time budget. Remember back to when you wanted to make your first big purchase? When Peta was a teenager, it was an electric bass guitar. She had just got her first job, but when she sat down to work out how many Saturday morning shifts it would take to cover the instrument's purchase price … it was sobering, to say the least. She wasn't getting a bass guitar that month. Possibly not even that year. Her teenaged-self learned to understand the value of time.

As adults, we know logically that time is our most precious resource. Once it's gone, we can never earn it back. Yet many academic writers make the mistake of treating time as if it's stretchy, or at least malleable, roughly 'guestimating' how long they'll need to invest to reach their major writing project goals. They tend to bank on 'best case scenarios' being the norm, opening themselves up to further risk. And they neglect to factor in contingency, as if there's a time credit card they can whip out of their back pocket if they find themselves overcommitted.

When you take out a major loan, the bank typically first makes you assess how much you could realistically spare in your weekly expenditure. It's the same for setting deadlines in a major writing project. First establish exactly how much writing time you have, and what that time is realistically 'worth' in terms of output. To set realistic goals for a major writing project, a writing time budget helps you get real, fast. When Peta runs Thesis Boot Camps, she provides participants with templates to help them work out their budgets.

You can create your own time budget with the following steps:

Define your 'units of currency': How much writing, editing or polishing can you get done in a set, measurable 'chunk' of time? When Peta was writing the first draft of her PhD she knew that she could get about 250 words out in 25 minutes on a bad day, twice as much on a really good day. (See next section, 'The Pomodoro Technique', for why she chose 25 minutes.) Always take the bad day as you baseline, because everything above that is a bonus and not to be relied upon. Doing the maths, '25 mins @ 250 words' became her unit of currency. Yours might be higher or lower, there are no 'right' answers but there are answers that are correct for you.

By regularly tracking your outputs, you'll create a baseline for your own units. Establish your baseline as early as you can in the life of the project. You might have to tweak it a little bit as you get more experienced (and therefore go faster), or you tackle more difficult material (and therefore go slower).

Establish your spending habits: 'Financial Advice 101' often recommends that you track and record all expenditure for a set period, that is long enough to factor in regular bills and pay days (often one month). Writing down everything helps you see what you actually spend, and what you spend it on, rather than what you think you spend. These can be very different things.

Newport argues that recording the way we spend our time can similarly lead to powerful insights about what's currently possible and what *could be* possible (2016, 221–232). As an initial exercise, try noting down how each half hour of your day is spent, from waking to sleeping, over the course of a full week. It may seem tedious, but a little effort in the short term will pay dividends in the long run.

After the week, ask yourself:

- When you factor in all your other commitments, how much time do you *really* spend writing?
- Were there periods during your day that had been reserved for writing but other things encroached?
- Does the reality match up with what you had convinced yourself you were investing in your writing? Or have you over- or underestimated?

Balance the books: Now that you know the amount of time you actually spend on writing during a week, tally up how many 'units of writing time currency' that represents.

That will give you a reliable estimation of what you can expect to produce (e.g., ten hours a week, at 500 words an hour = 5,000 first draft words). Compare it with any existing writing goals or deadlines for a clear picture of whether it is realistic to achieve those aims at your current level of investment.

Factor in contingency: It's now time to finalise your budget. Because life always throws unexpected things at us, factor in contingency before you set things in stone. Experienced project managers usually recommend assuming you'll get between 10–25% less done than you've calculated.

Perhaps your time budget looks good, and you can proceed with renewed confidence from your diligent data-gathering exercise. Alternatively, it may now look impossible to get that chapter done this month. Do you need to give more time to writing, or do you need to negotiate different deadlines?

The Pomodoro technique

One of the easiest ways to identify your 'unit' of time is the Pomodoro technique. This method of time management allows you to break large tasks into smaller, digestible chunks by only spending 25 minutes at a time on them, with five-minute breaks in between.

The person who came up with the idea of the Pomodoro technique – Francesco Cirillo – needed a device to keep track of his 25-minute work sessions. The nearest thing he had to hand was a kitchen timer shaped like a tomato – a *pomodoro* (Cirillo 2018, 2020). The word is now synonymous with describing 25-minute productivity bursts.

Let's say you have a significant task to accomplish today, such as, drafting a section of a chapter. You can plan to 'write 1,000 words of chapter today'. Or, you could divide your time up like the chart in Table 3.2.

During a Pomodoro, you don't need to type furiously fast. Just try to write steadily, at whatever pace you are comfortable with. Keep going without taking a break or switching tasks during that time, because after all, 'it's only 25 minutes'. At around the 15-minute mark, you might feel yourself starting to tire, but you can tell yourself 'it's only another ten minutes', which is easier to power through than 'it's only another few hours'. You can look forward to that five-minute break, you can reward yourself with a chat to your colleagues who share the office, or a coffee, or whatever works for you.

You might get to the end of a Pomodoro and find you were halfway through expressing a thought, and feel disappointed that you need to stop. That's great! If

Table 3.2 Using the Pomodoro Technique

Time allocated	Activity
25 minutes	Focused writing (250 words)
5 minutes	Break, refill water bottle
25 minutes	Focused writing (250 words)
5 minutes	Break, chat to office buddy
25 minutes	Focused writing (250 words)
5 minutes	Break, time to stretch
25 minutes	Focused writing (250 words)
20–30 minutes	Extended break, think about next task/section

you stop where you know exactly how to start again, and can't wait to get back into it, then you will fly straight back into that momentum after the break. You can scribble yourself a note about where you'll start next time, if you're worried you'll forget. This is also true for your whole day's writing. If you can, finish every writing session at an easy re-entry point. Starting the next session will be much less daunting.

Smaller units of writing are easier to slot into your days, and they help you to regularly achieve writing successes. Even if you can only find time in your budget for one Pomodoro a day, you will start to feel that writing is 'just one of the things I do, like answering emails or commuting to the office', rather than a big, mysterious, impossible, overwhelming task. If you aren't writing every day, a Pomodoro to warm you up will help you get back into the groove, which is particularly useful for part-time students who might only get to work on their writing one or two days a week.

Find a timer that works for you. Peta likes to adapt the number of minutes in each block. She finds 55-minute sessions more effective for editing. Some people find a shorter period is all they can reliably manage between children's interruptions. Katherine likes to build a playlist that lasts for exactly 25 minutes. It begins with an upbeat 'get started song', and when the music stops, it's time to take a break. You can use software that also tracks achievements, like Tomighty (that might help with 'Tracking your progress'); that produces white noise, like Noisli; or that help block other distracting apps, like Forest (these latter two will also help with avoiding the distractions discussed in 'Getting in the writing zone' in Chapter 9). Or you can use the timer on your phone, or even an old fashioned kitchen timer (even one that looks like a tomato!)

Now that you have a time budget mindset, you can go about building a schedule.

Making a schedule

The least effective strategy for getting everything done, is trying to do it all at once. During the day described in Chapter 2, the person wasn't able to focus on any one task, and became less effective overall. It's an understandable situation. There are a thousand things to do and everyone wants something from you. You become *reactive* to events. This is a trap you want to avoid. Why? It brings 'switch costs': every time you switch activities you have to change gears mentally and intellectually (Leroy 2009; Oberauer 2002). That change incurs a cost – time. And if you switch frequently through the day, the costs add up.

We therefore suggest you separate your tasks to structure your time. Before beginning the week, outline a clear schedule for yourself that you can stick to. Decide, for example, that Monday until lunch will be your class admin, and *only* your class admin. You won't feel guilty about answering email and not writing your thesis because you are planning to answer emails. Monday afternoon will be reviewing data and notes to make a writing plan for yourself for Tuesday. Then, Tuesday until lunch is strictly for writing. You aren't trying to do anything else during that time and you've given yourself permission to not feel guilty about the unanswered emails and other people's priorities, because that is your space during the week that is solely dedicated to writing. And so on.

When you structure your week this way, you aren't chaotically multitasking. You're not always reacting to other people's deadlines. And you're not feeling like you have no control over your time. If you work in a noisy office or at close proximity to a supervisor who needs things from you throughout the week, we know it is not easy to set firm boundaries and say 'no' to others. If you work at home with caring responsibilities, again you are likely to have lots of interruptions unless you can get someone else to take responsibility for some of the time so you can focus. But if you want to get your thesis finished, it is essential to have some uninterrupted time.

Take your plan and put it into a diary or daily planner. Use your time budget skills to map the tasks onto your time.

Making a project plan

Once you have reviewed your goals, worked out your realistic output levels, decided how you will track your progress, and made a regular schedule, then you have all the tools you need to build a robust, effective project plan for your final year of the PhD.

A project plan can be on a single sheet of paper, a whiteboard, or you can use fancy project management software. Some universities require a version of your project plan for an annual progress meeting. We recommend making a new project plan at least once per year. If you haven't made a new plan since you went through an early approvals process, now is definitely the time for it. Your new plan should include a review of the previous plan, factoring in where thing went awry in the past and incorporating the lessons learned.

Your plan should include:

- A description of what the project's deliverables are. In any project, these are the 'products' you will deliver to your client. For a PhD thesis, they are usually the chapters you will hand in to your supervisor.
- The tasks required to complete each deliverable product.
- The relevant approval processes. How will each deliverable be judged to be 'finished'? Will supervisors look at it in an order and decide, or will you all meet to discuss it?
- Timeframes for each task and deliverable. Include any external deadlines, such as a visa expiry, a baby's due date, a new employment contract start.
- The resources you will need to fulfil the project plan. Include budget, tools, software, desk space, travel funding, expert input.
- The assumptions you are making in the plan. For example, the plan works only if you don't need to take sick leave unexpectedly and your final experiments go smoothly. Factor in annual leave and conference travel.
- Foreseeable risks to the plan. Identify what might go wrong, and thus what you can put in place ahead of time to mitigate these risks. As recommended earlier, we encourage you to build in 10–25% of contingency buffer.

The internet is also full of excellent resources for project management. It's worth seeking these out to manage specific challenges you might be facing in your particular research project. For academic project management, we recommend the The Thesis Whisperer blog (2010–present) and the blog on Raul Pacheco-Vega's website (Pacheco-Vega, 2009–present); Katherine also regularly posts productivity advice on her blog, Research Degree Insiders (Firth, 2012–present, and you'll find more tips for overcoming writers block and 'making words happen' in Parts II and III of this book.

You're not imagining it

To sum up: it's hard. It's *really, really, hard*. There is no point pretending it's easy. The end of a PhD is the most intellectually exhausting task many students have ever undertaken, and many find it emotionally, socially, and financially draining. Nonetheless, most people find a way through this stage and do successfully complete their thesis and pass. Putting in place systems that acknowledge the challenge and realistically plan for it, though, will help you survive this stage in the best shape possible.

References

Cirillo, Francesco. 2018. *The Pomodoro Technique: The Life-Changing Time-Management System*. London: Penguin Random House.

Firth, Katherine. 2012–present. Research degree insiders blog. https://researchinsiders.blog

Francesco, Cirillo. 2020. "Short bio." About Francisco Cirillo. Accessed April 7. https://francescocirillo.com/pages/francesco-cirillo

Freestone, Peta. 2018. "You and writing deadlines: BFFs or toxic frenemies?" Dr. Peta Freestone blog. www.petafreestone.com/2017/09/06/your-writing-deadlines/

Leroy, Sophie. 2009. "Why is it so hard to do my work? The challenge of attention residue when switching between work tasks." *Organizational Behavior and Human Decision Processes* 109, no. 2: 168–181. doi:10.1016/j.obhdp.2009.04.002

Mewburn, Inger. 2010–present. The Thesis Whisperer blog. https://thesiswhisperer.com

Newport, Cal. 2016. *Deep Work: Rules for Success in a Distracted World*. New York: Grand Central.

Oberauer, Keith. 2002. "Access to information in working memory: Exploring the focus of attention." *Journal of Experimental Psychology: Learning, Memory, and Cognition* 28, no. 3: 411–421.

Pacheco-Vega, Raul. 2018. "Planning the timeline and progress of your doctoral dissertation (or Masters/undergraduate thesis)." Raul Pacheco-Vega, PhD blog. www.raulpacheco.org/2018/10/planning theses/

Pacheco-Vega, Raul. 2009–present. Raul Pacheco-Vega, PhD blog. www.raulpacheco.org/blog/

Rapp, Charles A. and Richard J. Goscha. 2011. *The Strengths Model: A Recovery-oriented*. New York: Oxford University Press.

4 Working with your strengths and weaknesses

In Chapter 2, we discussed the challenges you have to face when getting through the final stages of any project, and how for a PhD there are several factors that can potentially magnify that difficulty. How you experience the PhD 'project crunch' period will be affected by your approach and your preferred working style. Many of us don't have a clear grasp of what our preferred working styles actually are, though we may have an instinctive gut-feel preference that manifests in unconsciously-developed working habits. It's a good idea to consciously reflect, and then choose to play to your strengths. Let's explore that.

What kind of researcher are you?

To conclude this part of the book, we encourage you to think reflectively and critically about your own strengths and weaknesses, as a researcher, as a writer, and, importantly, as someone who is focusing a large part of their life on making a contribution to their chosen scholarly field. Everyone will have different approaches and strengths when it comes to writing a thesis. Everyone will find their own individual difficulties towards the end of the project. Being aware of your strengths and weaknesses will help you target those things you want to work on, and to use what you do well to get your thesis written.

Let's look at a few examples.

Meet Juliette. Juliette is well into her third year of a PhD in cyber security. Juliette has a data set that can only be described as gargantuan. Around a year ago, Juliette developed an algorithm that is ground-breaking in her field, but it needed a lot of testing and validation. Now past the two-and-a-half-year mark, Juliette was concerned about how little of the actual thesis she had to show, given the endless hours she spends in the lab. Her supervisor encouraged her to keep collecting more data.

Juliette has mixed feelings. She loves the research process and adores her overall project, but is uncomfortable about how little of it has appeared in writing. Juliette knows she has to present chapter drafts at a progress review next month. She's looking at her voluminous data and doesn't even know where she should begin writing. She doesn't enjoy the writing, and would rather go back to the lab.

Now meet Wei-Qin. Wei-Qin is a creative practice researcher who is using mixed modalities to create a series of art installations. Her art is brilliant and has attracted the attention of industry peers. Wei-Qin is constantly shifting and changing both her approach to her art and the conceptual framework that she is using for her PhD, upon which her thesis ultimately needs to be written. As a result, her methodology and literature review chapters are never finished, and in fact often have to be started again.

Wei-Qin's supervisor is supportive of Wei-Qin's work and recognises its brilliance, but has grown frustrated with her ability to move forward. She thinks Wei-Qin is a profound perfectionist and has grave doubts about Wei-Qin ever finishing. Wei-Qin feels like the ultimate imposter, painfully aware that while *talking* about her work is no problem, the lack of words on a page is frightening.

Finally, meet Nasim. Nasim is also a final year PhD, working in political science. Nasim's research is focused on the Arab Spring of 2010. Nasim has written a great deal of his thesis and is deeply engaged in his topic. Lately Nasim and his supervisor are really getting on each other's nerves. Nasim is always wanting to push ahead, get the next chapter written as soon as possible. His supervisor believes Nasim is impatient and needs to go back and strengthen his theoretical framework.

Nasim frequently has the 'so what?' discussion with his supervisor. He'll write a draft based on original research and what he believes the data is saying, hand it to his supervisor and receive feedback like, 'this is all interesting, but so what? Why am I reading it? What does it tell us?' Nasim has had this note so many times and he is frustrated because his work is so obviously timely and relevant. No one has ever given Nasim practical advice on editing his own writing. He follows his supervisor's individual line edits and mark-ups of grammar and typos. He doesn't know what else he could be doing to edit the draft in a way that will satisfy his supervisor.

What are the strengths and weaknesses of these approaches?

In these three case studies, Juliette, Wei-Qin, and Nasim all have strengths and weaknesses in how they approach work, but none of the three are fully aware of how they can 'leverage' their strengths, in corporate speak.

These are three types of PhD students that we encounter a lot.

Juliette is an **Explorer**. She is incredibly deep into her research and rarely comes up for air. If there was no limit on time or budget, she would remain buried in data and research forever. She has a singular engagement with her own research and has amassed more original research than anyone she knows, but the endless research she has gathered is drowning her. She is so engaged in the problems she is solving that she has lost sight of what other scholars in her field have contributed, and that makes it hard to contextualise her research and explain why it matters. In turn, that makes it harder for her to write up her research.

Wei-Qin is a **Methodologist**. She has put an enormous amount of thought and energy into the *how* of what she is doing, in reference to peers and scholars in her industry. She is determined to get her creative practice absolutely right, so her scope and limitations are constantly evolving, and she is reluctant to write because she doesn't want to commit to a particular position before she is ready. But this makes it hard to move on from refining her method to recording her results and analysis.

Nasim is an **Activist**. He is a person whose scholarly and professional practice is driven by the need to *act* and continually deliver on something, rather than just describe

Working with your strengths and weaknesses 51

it and think about it. He has tremendous energy and willpower and has no trouble creating huge bodies of writing. But while creating new material is straightforward for him, knowing what to do with it next is not. His supervisor keeps pushing him to communicate why his research matters, without explaining how to achieve that. So each draft only yields a repeat of the previous feedback.

All three have their own strengths and weaknesses. All three are also encountering problems that arise from different kinds of excess and scarcity. Juliette has too much data and not enough written analysis of what she has discovered. Wei-Qin has too much awareness of how she could improve her practice, but not enough progress towards completing a draft. Nasim has too much first draft material, and not enough structure to explain why his research matters.

What sorts of things can Juliette, Wei-Qin, and Nasim do to help themselves? If any of us had encountered any of these three, we'd likely ask them questions about their situation. We'd try to tease out where and how they position their research, and how what they *do* know can be developed and advanced through their writing.

For Juliette, she needs to get immersed into her writing the same way she gets immersed in her research. The advice in Chapter 9 'Getting words down' might be helpful here. Juliette might also wonder if a PhD thesis will actually take her professional career forward, or if she should just jump straight into industry and build more algorithms, so Chapter 13 'Do you actually want to finish the PhD' might also be useful.

For Wei-Qin, we recommend she works to define her scope more narrowly, and decide what she can continue to explore and what needs to wait for another project. So we would suggest Wei-Qin takes no more than an hour to go over the advice in 'Defining the project' from Chapter 1, to clarify her thesis question and answer, and then to build a pragmatic project plan to help build some momentum using the advice in Chapter 3 'Practical project management'.

For Nasim, we would be encouraging him to go back to his original research question and articulate the specific problem that first inspired him. From there, we would likely recommend he learn more about structural editing, perhaps using a process like writing some 'Tiny Texts' to identify his argument and its significance, and then adding in clear 'signposting' to explain how each part of the thesis is relevant. Chapter 10 'Making the thesis into a coherent work' will therefore be the most useful for him; though he might also benefit from Chapter 8 'Working with your supervisor'.

A strength-based approach is one where you focus on your strengths and advantages when facing a challenge, rather than your problems and deficiencies (Rapp and Goscha 2011). It is not to minimise or dismiss where improvements can be made in addressing a problem, but rather to draw attention first to what an individual can bring to a task. When a person is more consciously aware of their strengths, they can make a lot of progress intentionally building on them, as an emerging scholar and peer in their field.

Finding the 'I' in the thesis

You have probably been told at various points in candidature to keep a research journal, recording research notes, ideas, assumptions, and changes in thinking. We agree that it is a helpful strategy. We also recommended keeping writing journals in 'Tracking your progress' from Chapter 3.

In the final year of a PhD, it can be helpful to keep one further type of journal, or add some extra reflections to your current journaling practice. This final journal focuses on your overall approach to the PhD, how it has changed, and what you have learned from the experience that can be applied elsewhere.

We suggest the headings included in Table 4.1.

You will produce perhaps a maximum of one page per week, half of which are dot points. Feel free to make yours longer or shorter though, find what works for you each time.

With a structured exercise like this, you are more likely to regularly take the time and space to critically reflect on your own strengths and developments as a researcher, as a thinker, and as what recruiters call

Table 4.1 Keeping a research journal

Heading	Suggested length of entry	Frequency of entry
What happened this week?	Two paragraphs	Weekly
What did I learn?	Half page dot points	Weekly
What did I find difficult?	One paragraph	Weekly
What do I have to do next?	One paragraph	Weekly
What are my strengths as a researcher?	One page, dot points	Monthly
What kind of thinker am I?	Half page	Six-monthly

a professional 'knowledge worker'. Particularly during the final year of a PhD, all your time and attention can be consumed by thesis, thesis, thesis. It is difficult to carve out breathing space to think about what it is that you are actually doing (and are able to do) that can be usefully applied beyond the content of your thesis.

And yet, once the thesis is finished, it is this other stuff – who you are as a thinker and actor – that people are going to want to know about most of all, much more so than the minutiae of your thesis. We want you to focus on that, too.

In conclusion

If specific aspects of your PhD are a particular struggle for you, don't despair. Almost everyone hits a brick wall at a similar point, even if that brick wall isn't the same for everyone. You might be more of a conceptual explorer like Juliette, a process-driven maker like Wei-Qin, or an action-oriented writer like Nasim. All of these approaches have a lot to offer the task at hand, even though they are so different, and even if they sometimes feel like a block rather than a benefit.

You can survive the PhD

The end of the PhD is difficult because there is no longer any room to hide from the 'big questions' about your project: what it is you are actually doing, what it is you are saying that is original, and why it matters. In the years you have been working on your PhD, you might have been able to defer these questions until 'later' or 'when you have done more research'. That is no longer possible.

You have a fast diminishing timeline. Things like funding and visas are running out. Plus there's all the usual chaos of trying to wrap up a major project. But know that there are healthy and unhealthy ways for you to approach finishing a PhD, along with all its requisite sub-tasks. In Part II, we discuss the importance of self-care and strategies for smoothing your path to the finish line, whilst confronting the realities that lie ahead. We discuss ways of identifying your own strengths-based approach and how to identify patterns in your thinking that can help you make progress, even when other students may be managing things completely differently.

You may need to think hard and creatively about how to work on areas where feedback is telling you that you can improve. But don't diminish what you are awesome at – your strengths are what will carry you through to the finish line.

Reference

Rapp, Charles A. and Richard J. Goscha. 2011. *The Strengths Model: A Recovery-Oriented Approach to Mental Health Services*. New York: Oxford University Press.

Part II
Focusing on the person

A PhD is a logistical project, a piece of writing and, as Kamler and Thomson (2007) have argued, identity work. You don't only have to produce expert-level research, you also have to become an expert researcher in order to pass.

What's more, the majority of the expert-level work you need to produce is done by you alone. You do the researching, you do the writing, and you do a lot of the editing. You need to advocate for the project with stakeholders, and explain your thinking to your supervisors. The final PhD is judged on your ability to be a convincing researcher to your examiners.

The final stages of writing the PhD can feel isolating. Some students have been writing and working mostly on their own for the whole degree. Others are facing the challenge of working individually for the first time, as they exit the lab or return from fieldwork. Healthy self-management and relationship management are even more important as you enter this intensive writing phase.

This part of the book has the most variation on whether the exact advice we give you will be right for your circumstances. We thought really hard about everything we put in here, and we think the high-level principles are helpful for most people – regardless of your country, university, or personal circumstances.

In this part of the book, we debunk some myths about personal effectiveness that hinder rather than help students. Then we give advice for when you are feeling 'stuck' and are not sure how to save yourself and get moving again. Finally, we discuss working with the other really significant person in the PhD project: your supervisor. We offer insights for effective relationships both with good supervisors and challenging supervisors.

Reference

Kamler, Barbara and Pat Thomson. 2007. "Rethinking doctoral writing as text work and identity work." in Bridget Somekh and Thomas A. Schwandt (eds), *Knowledge Production: Research Work in Interesting Times*. 166–179. Routledge: London.

5 'No pain, no gain' and other unhelpful myths

During a PhD, you often have choices about how and when you work, especially as you start to focus more on writing rather than research. You can work from anywhere, at any time, which means you have to make your own decisions about whether you want to work evenings and weekends; whether you work from home or in an office or café; as well as what software you use. Some of these choices can be made without much reflection, reacting to your circumstances, or based on academic cultural norms. Some of these 'normal' ways of working are based on unhelpful myths, so it's worth reflecting on whether you really do have to work all the hours. Your choices of how, when and how much to work have potentially big impacts on your physical and mental health, which in turn impact your ability to finish your PhD.

Myth 1: All stress is created equal

It is becoming more widely and openly acknowledged that undertaking a PhD in contemporary academia can be chronically stressful *in itself* (Levecque et al. 2017; Evans et al. 2018; Stubb, Pyhältö and Lonka 2011). For late-stage PhD students in particular, chronic stress is an unfortunately common phenomenon.

While deadlines and milestones can be a way to induce short-term 'good stress' to help you perform at your best, being chronically stressed over sustained periods is not helpful (Selye 1975). Chronic (ongoing) stress is likely to hinder your ability to prioritise, focus, and access the higher cognitive functions needed to synthesise years of research into a written thesis.

It's a dangerous idea to think of chronic stress as something to be accepted as part of the job, as an illustration of 'working hard', or even as a badge of honour to be worn in stoic solidarity among peers. Yes, short-term discomfort is common while you struggle to develop new concepts, write difficult sections of the thesis, or prepare a crucial presentation. The sense of unease when doing something challenging is critical to improve your skills and to get better at your work – it's known in the psychology, business and education fields as 'deliberate practice' (Ericsson 2004).

But it's important to separate the context-specific discomfort of deliberate practice from pervasive anxiety, distress, or exhaustion. Chronic stress is *not* a correlate of success, nor is 'no pain, no gain' a required precondition for finishing a PhD. The next four 'myths' unpack specific ways you might reduce chronic stress created by the PhD itself.

Myth 2: The more hours, the more productivity

How many hours did you work today? What about the past week? We often talk to PhD students who feel that unless they're working six or seven days per week they're 'not working hard enough' or they're 'slacking off'. It could be a feeling they've developed individually, or it could be something that has been imposed by the culture of a department or research group. Yet more and more studies show that we simply can't be productive for the endless work weeks that are often the norm in academic settings.

Alex Soojung-Kim Pang, now a visiting scholar at Stanford University and director of his own Silicon Valley consultancy, was inspired by his PhD experience. The title of his book neatly captures the argument he makes, *Rest: Why You Get More Done When You Work Less*. Not only are breaks crucial to avoiding chronic stress and burnout, it's also an essential condition for making the sorts of creative breakthroughs that are the hallmarks of great research.

We therefore urge you to consider committing to a five-day work week. Six at absolute most. Even if you are doing a PhD part time on top of a full-time job, working seven days per week is not sustainable, and it won't serve you or your research.

You are likely to only be able to do focused writing for two–four hours a day on average. Adding on extra hours at the desk is usually counter-productive, whether you feel ahead or behind. Even people who are reaching their research, writing and editing goals faster than their allotted work time often feel like they need to spend more hours working. Resist the urge.

Myth 3: Dedicated PhD students don't take holidays

You should be taking holidays. Now we're talking about serious downtime. Actual vacations. Regular breaks and longer planned periods away from your thesis are not only beneficial to you, they'll help you finish your PhD more efficiently. Plan in advance, and in consultation with the various stakeholders in your project, to step away from the PhD for at least a week during the next few months. Yes, a whole week. Maybe two. Get away from your usual workspace and spend time with your family, friends or partner. Sleep in. Bake cakes or do the gardening. Catch up on all the movies you missed and chill out.

If you're motivated and working regularly over the final year, there's absolutely no need to work *all* the time. Remember that PhD student contracts have annual leave built into them for a reason: to avoid a one-way trip to burnout. And if you need longer because you are feeling deep exhaustion, seek help, and consider an intermission of studies to stop the clock on your candidature. Burnout is a medical condition, not a sign of weakness.

We'll say it again: give yourself actual breaks. You've earned them!

Myth 4: Self-care is only for social media influencers

In the late stages of a PhD, many students feel time-poor, under pressure, stressed and tired. Self-care activities such as good nutrition, exercise and social connection may have slipped down the priority list. But we believe that the final year of candidature is one of the most important times to look after yourself. Self-care is not just bubble baths and candles, it is the real work of taking responsibility for your health (Lorde, 1988).

If you undertook an assessment of your wellbeing at this point, how would you rate it compared to other times in your life? Have you been able to maintain a balance between the various demands and the things you need to do to stay healthy? Consider how you would assess yourself against five major indicators of wellbeing: ergonomics, exercise, diet, sleep, and mental health.

Ergonomics: The more time you spend intensively working on your thesis, the more mindful you need to be of how your furniture and equipment setup impacts your body.

- Is your posture neutral, comfortable and balanced? Or are you slumped over your keyboard, feeling strain in your back or neck?
- What about your wrists? Do they need extra support?
- Does anything need to change to ensure you're not doing yourself physical damage?

If you have a workspace at your university, there may be ergonomics specialists on staff who you can make an appointment with to have your workspace assessed. If you work from home or elsewhere, consider simple fixes that can go a long way to avoiding strain.

- If your main computer is a laptop, you may wish to consider using a separate keyboard, mouse or monitor to reduce strain.
- Have your screen at eye height, for example by using a riser, or even a shoebox or a stack of big books.
- Be sure to take regular breaks from your screen to rest your eyes and stretch.
- Regularly vary your posture. Sit, stand, lie down, change chairs.

- Does your workspace have enough light? If not, add a desk lamp.
- Even if you don't use an ergonomic office chair, use cushions, lumbar support and footstools to reduce strain on your body.

Exercise: We're told constantly about the merits of physical exercise, both in terms of general health and for mood-boosting endorphins. Yet, despite knowing logically that exercise is good for us, we can underestimate its potential and importance, especially during the periods we most need its benefits! There's good reason why we have 'active' breaks at Thesis Boot Camps, from yoga to guided walks. Many participants are surprised at how much these sessions boost their concentration levels and sense of wellbeing so that they can get even more writing done.

Any movement-based activity will give you benefits including improved mood, clearer thinking, and counteracting the physical challenges of sitting at a desk for long periods (World Health Organization, 2020). Movement is really effective for reducing ongoing thesis stress too.

Pick whatever type of exercise that you can do on a regular basis, and don't let thesis busyness get in the way. Going for a run, lifting weights, playing team sports or practicing yoga count, but so do walking the dog, dancing in your living room, or doing some gardening.

Find something that works for your time, physical capacity, and situation. Your body and mind will thank you. Your thesis will, too.

Nutrition: We recommend making sure your nutrition is as good as it can be at this time. Just like a computer can't run without electricity or battery, your brain can't run without food. Skipping meals or forgetting whole food groups (like protein or vegetables) because you are busy makes it harder to stay energised and think clearly. Looking after your nutrition will ensure you function optimally, keep your immune system firing, and help you best tackle your thesis.

For some people, cooking and baking become a form of relaxation during their PhD years. Katherine found it helped her to get away from the desk and give her thinking time while her hands were busy with chopping, simmering, and stirring. Not everyone has time to relax while cooking. Peta relied on a tried and tested bunch of websites about eating well to a budget and reverted to online shopping to save time. Do you need to put similar hacks in place to ensure you are eating regularly and meeting your nutritional needs?

Sleep: You may have seen the ads warning you that driving without enough sleep is as dangerous as driving drunk (e.g. Traffic Accidents Commission, 2020, National Sleep Foundation, 2020). That's because the impacts of not getting enough sleep include:

- Difficulty focusing, shortened attention span.
- Slower reaction times.
- Poor concentration and reduced alertness.
- Reduced awareness of the environment and situation.
- Daydreaming or wandering/disconnected thoughts.
- Increased likelihood of mentally 'stalling' or fixating on one thought.
- Increase in errors.

Getting enough sleep is crucial to your ability to perform at your best.

The PhD is a marathon, not a sprint. When writing undergraduate essays, you may have got away with pulling the odd all-nighter or two, but you cannot burn the midnight oil consistently for years and still maintain your ability to focus. If you're not getting enough sleep, try to put seven–nine hours of sleep into your time budget if you possibly can (see 'Create a writing time budget' in Chapter 3).

Mental health: As we said earlier, the chronic stressors of doing a PhD can be bad for your mental health, or exacerbate existing mental health issues.

Are you feeling anxious about completing your thesis? Is it having an impact on other areas of your life? Or are there family, work or personal matters getting in the way of you thinking clearly? If you're experiencing mental health challenges, please talk to someone. Remember, no matter how bad you might feel, or how important it is for you to feel like you can cope … going it alone is rarely the solution. Seeking help is *not* a sign of weakness. Reach out to friends, family, university counselling services, private counselling, and/or your doctor.

Most universities offer counselling services for students to make appointments for one-to-one confidential counselling, often for free or a nominal fee. Counsellors can help you develop strategies to manage mental health challenges, as well as giving you a safe space to talk about your thoughts or feelings.

Everyone should also think about how to proactively build up their mental health at this time. For example, you could try a meditation practice, which gets you to take some time out of each day for a bit of calm. Many university health and wellbeing services offer workshops in stress management and relaxation, and university sports services often offer yoga, tai chi, and other exercise modes that include meditation. Similarly, we know lots of busy academics who swear by mindfulness apps, such as Headspace, that provide short meditations on your phone. Find the strategy that works for you. Investing time in your mental wellness will be time well spent.

Myth 5: Deadlines are always motivating

We discussed 'Goal setting' in Chapter 3 as a crucial aspect of managing your PhD project. Here, we want to look at the risks in setting unrealistic goals.

Have you ever missed a writing deadline? Missed one in the past few months? Maybe even a few of them? Crucially, have any of these been self-imposed deadlines? If so, it's probably time to reassess your relationship with your writing targets: a 'health check' for the way you set writing goals. Peta calls these problematic goals 'deadline frenemies' (Freestone 2018).

In the early days of the PhD, it's easy to shrug off writing tasks as they dozily hum in the background like bumble bees. They can be rescheduled. There are weeks, months, even years, left on the journey. You'll pick up the slack later. It'll be fine.

But there will come a time when things get serious (the project 'crunch' stage, Chapter 2). The clock is ticking on your candidature. It's possibly also ticking on funding, visas, publications, job applications, and on all that 'life stuff' that continues to happen while you tackle your research. By now, it might seem that those tasks that were once cute bumblebees have been replaced with a nest of wasps. Angry wasps. Furious sting-machines dive-bombing you from all directions.

What's your relationship with deadlines? While there is an infinite spectrum of experiences, for the sake of brevity, here's two extremes:

You and your deadlines have a harmonious, mutually beneficial relationship, where you both feel confident in each other. You address minor setbacks swiftly and your relationship recovers, even strengthens. Step-by-step, you work together to progress your thesis until it sprouts wings and flies off (wasp-free) into the happily-ever-achieved sunset.

Or, you and your deadlines seem to start off on the right foot. Everything is so exhilarating and rewarding that you rush headlong into making all sorts of plans before you've considered your other commitments. Then, after those first heady days, things begin to change. Due dates swing by and you find yourself standing your deadlines up. The first time, it doesn't seem like a big deal. But the second occasion? And the third? Before you know it, every time you bump into your deadlines, you can't bear the way they glare at you in judgement, making you feel even more terrible for not holding up your end of the bargain. Guilt starts to weigh you down, possibly so much that you start going well out of your way to avoid facing your deadlines. Things might get so toxic that you want to give up on your thesis altogether.

If your relationship with deadlines sounds anything like the second scenario, even occasionally, you may have developed some unhelpful habits when it comes to goal-setting. Peta readily admits she did during her PhD, and many people share similar experiences with us when we run Thesis Boot Camps and other writing workshops. (Related: Introduction 'Why we wrote this book'; Chapter 13 'Do you actually want to finish the PhD?')

On top of the other stressors PhD students face, psychologists have long known that certain goal-setting behaviours can increase the risk of mental health problems. When Peta was designing Thesis Boot Camp back in 2012, she approached psychology researcher Dr Helen Street (2011) who had been studying this phenomenon for years, including in PhD students. Peta learned from Helen's work that the link between goal-setting styles and mental health could become particularly problematic when we place conditions on what happens if we do or don't achieve those goals, such as 'I'll be happy when I finish my PhD'; 'I'll avoid disaster if I achieve a draft by June'.

In our work with students, we've observed again and again that setting deadlines and missing them over an extended period of time leaves students frustrated at best, and at worst frightened that they won't be able to finish their thesis. That's when those other horrible 'f' words creep in, like 'fraud' and 'failure'. (If you have these feelings, see Chapter 6 'Your harshest critic' for strategies to deal with them.)

In short: setting yourself deadlines can be motivating and provide structure and discipline to finish the thesis. However, setting yourself writing goals that you often don't achieve can do more harm than good – to your research project, and to your mental health.

If you're experiencing missed-deadline-stress, we urge you to examine the way you set your writing targets, or any other milestones you have the ability to negotiate. It could make a big improvement to how you feel about your writing, and have a positive influence on your day-to-day wellbeing. In turn, that helps your writing projects.

References

Ericsson, K. Anders. 2004. "Deliberate practice and the acquisition and maintenance of expert performance in medicine and related domains." *Academic Medicine* 79, no. 10: S70–S81.

Evans, Teresa M., Lindsay Bira, Jazmin Beltran Gastelum, L. Todd Weiss, and Nathan L. Vanderford. 2018. "Evidence for a mental health crisis in graduate education." *Nature Biotechnology* 36, no. 3: 282.

Freestone, Peta. 2018. "You and Writing Deadlines: BFF or toxic frenemies?" Dr Peta Freestone website. www.petafreestone.com/2018/09/06/your-writing-deadlines/

Headspace. www.headspace.com/

Levecque, Katia, Frederik Anseel, Alain De Beuckelaer, Johan Van der Heyden, and Lydia Gisle. 2017. "Work organization and mental health problems in PhD students." *Research Policy* 46, no. 4: 868–879. doi:10.1016/j.respol.2017.02.008

Lorde, Audre. 1988 [2017]. "A burst of light: Living with cancer." in *A Burst of Light and Other Essays*. 40–135. Mineola, NY: Ixia.

National Sleep Foundation. 2020. "Drowsy Driving vs. Drunk Driving: How similar are they?" Accessed 7 April. https://www.sleepfoundation.org/articles/drowsy-driving-vs-drunk-driving-how-similar-are-they

Pang, Alex Soojung-Kim. 2018. *Rest: Why You Get More Done When You Work Less*. 2nd ed. London: Penguin.

Selye, Hans. 1975. "Confusion and controversy in the stress field." *Journal of Human Stress* 1, no. 2: 37–44.

Street, Helen. 2011. *Life Overload: Immediate Life-saving Strategies from a Stress Expert*. Sydney: Finch Publishing.

Stubb, Jenni, Kirsi Pyhältö, and Kirsti Lonka. 2011. "Balancing between inspiration and exhaustion: PhD students' experienced socio-psychological well-being." *Studies in Continuing Education* 33, no. 1: 33–50.

Traffic Accidents Commission. Accessed April 7. 2020. "Pillow – you can't fight sleep." TAC Campaigns Drowsy Driving. www.tac.vic.gov.au/road-safety/tac-campaigns/drowsy-driving

World Health Organization. Accessed April 7. 2020. "Physical activity and adults." Global Strategy on Diet, Physical Activity and Health. www.who.int/dietphysicalactivity/factsheet_adults/en/

6 Your harshest critic

Writing involves a transition from talking to acting, from preparing to delivering. Therefore, the **act of writing is a performance**, where you show the world what you have been doing all this time (Thomson and Kamler 2014). It is a performance of your scholarly identity, of the ground you claim for yourself in your field. That is true for all academic works, but it is at its most intense with a doctoral thesis because it is you making a claim to be considered a peer among the academic experts in your field. It's not only a statement about your research and what you know, it's a statement of who you are as an emerging scholar. It is big stuff. Critical, high-stakes stuff. Like all performances, it is conducted in public and thus open to evaluation. Psychologically, practically, and emotionally, writing for an audience has all the components of a performance: the need to 'get it right', concerns about deficiencies, and needing to worry about what other people will think.

However, this is only true when the writing is handed over to other people for them to read. Over and over, we see PhD students conflate the writing of a first draft with this much later stage. As a result, when they sit down to write the thesis, it is all too easy to be gripped by worry or avoid it altogether, and no words get written. Remember, your performance is only open to evaluation at a much later stage than the first draft.

So we want you to think of the first time you write about your research as more like a private rehearsal or practice session. An actor on opening night or the person in the grand final of a sporting competition isn't doing any of this for the first time. They did a lot of practice first, alone and with peers or coaches, before they found themselves in front of a live audience.

Of course there is still one person in the audience when you write the first draft, and they can be your harshest critic – yourself. You bring to your writing your critical mind, your high expectations of yourself. You bring the expectations, real or imagined, of your academic peers, your community, friends, family; as well as the desire to do justice to the research itself. You are the first person to read your writing on your topic and you will know your reaction to it immediately.

This is why it's important to reflect on that harsh critic's beliefs, self-talk, and actions.

Your practices or beliefs are likely to be influencing how you go about the work required to complete your PhD. That is not to say that other people or the structures and systems you are living and working within have not contributed to these unhelpful thoughts and habits. Slow, insidious beliefs can build up over a long time and manifest in self-sabotaging ways. But if they are internal, then the solutions can also be internal. Here we will discuss some of the more common of these problematic internal beliefs. If any of these feel familiar to you, we also offer a 'verdict' with practical advice on how to get unstuck and start moving again.

Imposter syndrome

When you started your PhD, it was fine to feel like you didn't know very much. After all, you understood the whole point of undertaking a doctorate was to discover more about a particular topic. But you were probably expecting that feeling of 'not knowing enough' to eventually go away. Wasn't there supposed to be a time when you looked around at your peers and felt like you spoke the same language, knew your field's canon just as well, had regular breakthroughs and made original scholarly contributions just like them? Weren't you supposed to feel like you belonged?

Instead, you may be having thoughts like:

> I still don't know what I'm doing. Everyone seems so smart … smarter than me! It looks easy for my colleague at the next desk, but I find everything a challenge. Maybe I'll never belong here. What will happen if others find out that I'm a fraud?

These unhelpful thoughts are called **Imposter Syndrome**. It's a well-known phenomenon in many industry and creative contexts, and it is ubiquitous among PhD students (Kearns 2015). The reasons seem obvious when you examine them. As a person doing a PhD, your strongest skills are asking critical questions and analysing situations to see how they could be improved. PhD students occupy a liminal space between students and academic staff (never entirely one, not quite the other), whilst being surrounded continually by competitive colleagues. It would actually be surprising if a characteristically thoughtful and inquisitive person did not look at themselves within that environment at some point and think: 'Am I really up to it?' Almost everyone has doubted themselves at some point, but this isn't the worrying Imposter Syndrome.

For some people, Imposter Syndrome shouts relentlessly through a megaphone night and day. Imposter Syndrome can exert itself most powerfully right at the point of writing, because committing your thoughts into words puts them out there for all to see ... and judge. It's the point at which, if you're already feeling you don't belong, you risk being exposed.

Verdict: Talk to other PhD students: you'll quickly realise you're not the only one who sometimes questions if they belong. Then train your eyes back on your own work. Write. Then write some more. It's one of the best ways to banish those feelings of Imposter Syndrome, because doing the thing you're there to do demonstrates why you're there!

A caveat: some people have Imposter Syndrome, which is internal. Other people have been told, explicitly or obliquely, that they aren't good enough to be a successful researcher. Women, People of Colour, people with disabilities, and people from working class backgrounds are just some of the cohorts of PhD students who might have been told they were a 'diversity hire', got lucky, or otherwise don't belong in the academy (Tulshyan 2016). If it's Imposter Syndrome, you can solve the issue. If it's bullying or exclusion, then you need different strategies. For example, Chapter 7 addresses bullying supervisors.

Perfectionism and procrastination

Having high standards, caring about details and striving to make things better are all strengths common to PhD students. These qualities are important for academic success. Perfectionism, however, is where your desire to get things exactly right overwhelms you, stopping you from doing work or making progress. Knowing you can't make it perfect, it's then all too easy to not even try. That leads to the common error of **mistaking perfectionism and procrastination for risk management**.

You may find yourself engaging in one of the most common acts of self-protection and preservation during a PhD: procrastination. **Procrastination** can involve tasks that give you a sense of achievement or belonging, tasks that are essential and useful if done in proportion: answering e-mails, applying for conferences, tutoring or doing research assistant work, helping junior colleagues in the lab, organising reading groups …. If you are doing all of these things, but never getting to the actual thing that is going to signal you're ready to join the scholarly community as an independent researcher – your thesis – then you need to reassess.

Back in 2009, veteran US radio presenter Ira Glass introduced the concept of 'the taste gap'. According to Glass, the 'taste gap' describes how, early in your career, there is a frustrating distance between the quality of work you'd like to produce and the work you actually produce. You've got 'killer taste', you know what you like, the work that's already out there that you think is top notch. But you can't yet achieve that in your own work.

How does the 'taste gap' manifest in PhD terms? You're reading high-impact publications by experts in the field, and you rightly think: 'I want my work to be of this quality'. After researching, conferencing, and thinking about these ideas for years, you understand their importance and complexity. But there is likely to be a big deficit between the compelling, insightful knowledge in your head, and the often unfocused version that initially appears on the page. You stand back and look at your first draft and think ... 'is that it? Is that all there is to it?' In that moment of panic, the answer that comes from your lizard brain is, 'yes, that's all there is, because you can't do this'. The writing is where you finally put your money where your mouth is, and you came up short. The experience fuels a fear that you can't write. You begin to assign a huge risk to writing, as though you are taking your life into your hands.

It is not a true risk. It's not 'all there is to it', or all you are capable of. It's unhelpful to compare your early PhD drafts to your favourite academic monograph or article. The text of your thesis may form the basis of publications, but it will substantially change during the editing process. More importantly, that published book you're comparing your writing to has been peer reviewed, had editor input, professional copy edits and proofreading. You will need to write more, and go through multiple rounds of edits to get your work to look like the published work of other scholars (see Chapters 10 'Making the thesis into a coherent work' and 11 'Making the words good').

So, what did Glass have to say about addressing the so-called 'taste gap'? The only way to close it is to do the work. In the case of the PhD thesis, to push through the discomfort and produce imperfect writing. Again. And again. Eventually, your knowledge, skills, and subsequent drafts will catch up to your taste. Avoiding writing to protect yourself from that uncomfortable 'taste gap' feeling you get when you read your first drafts absolutely will not make the work any better.

The truth is, avoiding writing your thesis is the real risk to your PhD.

Verdict: The only way to produce work of the highest quality is to practice doing the work ... again and again. Perfection is the enemy of progress. Check out Chapter 9, especially the section about the 'perfect sentence vortex' for practical techniques to get words on the page. Then start writing. And keep writing.

JOMA Syndrome

Another procrastination technique used by many late-stage PhD students to put off writing Peta calls **JOMA (Just One More Article) Syndrome**. Sometimes it's a symptom of Imposter Syndrome. But it can also be its very own condition. Gardiner and Kearns (2010) call this 'Readitis'.

'I haven't read enough yet' is one of the most common reasons we hear students give for why they can't begin writing their thesis, or tackle the next chapter. The 'yet' in that reason is very important. Why? It implies that they foresee a point in the future where they will feel they've indeed read everything needed. But we have some news for you: you may never feel you've read enough. We repeat: **you may never feel you've read enough**.

Every single week there will be papers or books published in your discipline. Some of these will even be relevant to the niche research area of your PhD. But it's not going to stop. This close to the end of your PhD, it's

Your harshest critic 79

unlikely you will find a magical article or book that unlocks something within you that allows you to go from feeling like writing is an uphill battle, to feeling like your words are water just pouring from a tap.

You know you have to confront the writing, that the chapters are not going away and the blank page isn't going to fill itself. In other people it is a distraction technique, but you might truly believe that, in your specific case, given the particular nature of your work and the unique juncture you are at with your thesis, you absolutely must read Just One More Article before you can start writing the chapter.

Liam had a moment of clarity in the final year of his PhD, stuck in an airport on the way home from a conference, he was complaining to a senior colleague about how he couldn't find any book that would shine a light on a central problem in his research. 'That's fantastic,' the other person said. 'That's the best problem to have. Don't you get it? *You* are writing the book you're looking for.'

You can start writing before you have all the answers (as we say in Chapter 9, sometimes the best strategy is 'Working it out by writing it out'). Once you start writing, you're going to be synthesising ideas and literature, and figuring out exactly where there might be a gap you need to fill. You'll be reading more, but as part of the writing process. The sooner you work that out, the sooner you'll be on your way to a complete thesis.

Verdict: Academia is an ongoing conversation. At some point, you're going to have to stop listening and start adding your voice. Trust yourself. You know more than you think. And what you don't know? You can go back and find as needed.

Aiming for an 'A' grade

There's a joke among researcher developers and supervisors. It goes like this:

Question: What do you call someone who submits an average, pedestrian PhD thesis?
Answer: Doctor.

Sure, that's a tongue-in-cheek over-simplification, but there's truth at its essence. Aside from the very few university medals or professional association prizes, there's no 'High Distinction' or 'A' grade waiting for you at the end of a PhD. There's a pass grade, or a request from the examiners to make corrections with time and guidance to then get a pass grade.

So don't **mistake your PhD for a coursework essay**. Unlike in your undergraduate or Master's days, you aren't receiving regular feedback in the form of grades to confirm you're on the right track. Instead, milestones are less defined, even amorphous. They're also spaced much more widely apart. You can go a whole year without having to submit any sort of formal work, such as a progress report, and even then it's usually on a pass or resubmit basis. All those 'A' grades that used to tell you that you were performing well are nowhere to be seen.

On the other hand, some students **mistake their PhD for their *magnum opus*** (great work). Many students believe they need to answer all the big problems with their PhD. They don't. Other students have a desire to 'save the world' with their PhD. They won't. Take a look at who wins Nobel Prizes, usually people many, many years out of their PhD.

'But', you say 'examiners will only pass my thesis if it's excellent!' That's not necessarily true. Experienced examiners are looking for you to take your first independent step along the long road of a research career, as studies of how examiners assess theses have shown time and again, for example, Mullins and Kiley's aptly-titled 'It's a PhD, not a Nobel Prize' (2002).

We encourage you to internalise the idea that while a PhD thesis needs to be a well-written document presenting an original contribution to your field, evidenced with soundly-conducted research, it does not need to be your *magnum opus*, which comes later in your research career.

Verdict: An average PhD is a pass-worthy PhD. You should check out some recent passed PhD theses from your university (talk to your librarian to find out how to find them at your institution) to see what the standard really is. You may be surprised to find that you are already closer to the standard than you had thought.

Avoiding failure

The fact that you're undertaking a PhD demonstrates that you are a good student. It doesn't matter if you followed a linear path from high school to here, or if your journey to the PhD contained more twists and turns, even stops and starts. At some point, you established a track record of academic achievement over a period of years. Therefore, **many PhD students find that being 'good' at academic activities has become part of their identity**. By succeeding again and again, the people in your life have probably also come to view you as intelligent and 'good at school'. If your identity is based on the idea of 'being smart equals always having academic successes', both you, and those around you, perceive of yourself as intellectually successful ... until you start to fail sometimes.

It is the nature of a PhD that you will experience failures. Experiments don't work. You can't find the data you expected. You don't understand a concept. The method doesn't fit. Your theory breaks down. Your journal article got rejected. Your supervisor returned your draft with a lot of red pen corrections. They are a normal part of research life.

Sometimes having academic set-backs might make you wonder if you are still smart. You might wonder if you have what it takes to pass. You wonder if, after all those years, and with the stakes now higher than they have ever been, you might fail at the whole PhD. **Fear of failure** sets in.

This is the issue with having a 'fixed mindset'. As Dweck has shown, our own beliefs about ourselves guide our behaviour. In her book *Mindset: The Psychology of Success* (2017), Dweck discusses the 'fixed mindset' versus the 'growth mindset' – two different ways individuals view learning that are evident from early childhood. When you have a 'fixed mindset', your conception of being smart or capable is static. You don't believe your qualities can change. So, after a series of setbacks, you might begin to believe that the PhD is too hard for you. On the other hand, a 'growth mindset' means you believe you can learn and improve. You view the challenges of your PhD as helping you to see where you need to grow, and you understand that facing each challenge and overcoming it helps you to do that growing.

If you find yourself believing that your smartness is static, you're likely taking a fixed mindset approach. You may fear that others also view you in the same way. Which means that you need to hide any setbacks you come up against, so that you can preserve the appearance of being smart and capable. If you don't fail at anything, you can at least still *seem* to belong. So it can feel like a good idea to avoid tough jobs, like writing, or give up after a few minutes of finding it hard.

Fortunately, Dweck's research demonstrates you can change your mindset. A growth mindset leads to a desire to learn – usually the urge that set you on the path to a PhD in the first place. Reconnecting with your curiosity or quest for knowledge can help you embrace challenges rather than avoid them.

Verdict: You are not your PhD, nor will your entire career be defined by your PhD. What's more, the one guaranteed way to fail a PhD is to not face the challenges and do the work. Keep exploring. Keep learning. Keep writing. That's what truly smart researchers do!

To summarise, you can get in your own way when it comes to trying to finish the PhD. The very nature of the PhD experience can encourage some of these internal reasons for feeling stuck. This is normal! You're not alone! These kinds of thoughts and feelings do not make you an outlier or less capable. If you get together with other PhD students, you will hear the same concerns from many other people in your situation.

The good news? Once you recognise what's going on, these struggles get easier to identify and quicker to resolve. Whichever of these internal reasons for feeling stuck you might be experiencing, the best solution is often to **just start writing and keep writing**. From where you are right now, you may not be able to see that writing could be the solution. But believe us, it usually is. The ultimate take home message is that writing may be difficult or scary, but *not* writing is a far riskier strategy. Keep going!

Conclusion

You often have more power over your thoughts and beliefs than you realise. Changing your attitude, even just realising that you are far from alone and many other students face very similar challenges, can be transformative.

'Feeling stuck' might be caused by internal factors. However, they can also be caused by external factors, as we discuss in the next chapter. Often it's a mix of both. The good news is that in most cases, the 'stuck' feeling is being caused by factors that can be unpacked and addressed. And that means it's possible to get unstuck, and start making progress again.

References

Dweck, Carol. 2017. *Mindset: The Psychology of Success*. 6th ed. London: Robinson.

Gardiner, Maria and Hugh Kearns. 2010. *Turbocharge Your Writing: How to Become a Prolific Academic Writer*. Adelaide: Flinders University.

Glass, Ira. 2009. "On Storytelling". Audio in video by David Shiyang Liu. 2011. "Ira Glass on Storytelling". https://vimeo.com/24715531. Transcript: Maria Popova. 2104. "The Taste Gap: Ira Glass on the Secret of Creative Success, Animated in Living Typography". Brain

Pickings. https://www.brainpickings.org/2014/01/29/ira-glass-success-daniel-sax/

Kearns, Hugh. 2015. *The Imposter Syndrome: Why Successful People Often Feel like Frauds*. Adelaide: ThinkWell.

Mullins, Gerry and Margaret Kiley. 2002. "'It's a PhD, not a Nobel Prize': How experienced examiners assess research theses." *Studies in Higher Education* 27, no. 4: 369–386. 10.1080/0307507022000011507.

Thomson, Pat and Barbara Kamler. 2014. *Helping Doctoral Students Write: Pedagogies for Supervison*. 2nd ed. Abingdon: Routledge.

Tulshyan, Ruchika. 2016. "What To Do When You're Called A 'Diversity Hire'". *Forbes*. www.forbes.com/sites/ruchikatulshyan/2016/10/18/what-to-do-when-youre-called-a-diversity-hire/

7 Getting unstuck

In the late stages of a PhD, many students will feel 'stuck'. We've worked with thousands of students in their final year who speak about their experience using words associated with restriction. They feel 'trapped' by the seemingly insurmountable amount of work left to do. They can't wait to 'escape' and move onto the next stage of their career. A thesis topic they once found so fascinating and full of promise has become something heavy that they have to drag around each day. The perception of being stuck or trapped is powerful. It can *feel* impossible to break. But it *isn't* impossible.

The previous chapter 'Your harshest critic' laid out some of the ways in which you might have become your own worst enemy. Not all reasons for feeling stuck or overwhelmed come from internal beliefs about yourself or arise from how you engage with your work. It's even harder when there are external factors putting pressure on you. Even the most positive and efficient person can find themselves waylaid by life.

We know that PhD students are likely to be at a life stage with more everyday complexity than their undergraduate days: financial or family care responsibilities, restrictions of international student visas, energy spent in paid employment, maintaining interpersonal relationships. And all on top of the demands of a PhD! Sometimes there are structural barriers, such as institutional policies that limit participation or are outright discriminatory. Such external factors can be challenging for any student, but sometimes they can become a perfect storm of circumstances, buffeting you with stress until 'just getting through the day' is a challenge, let alone writing a thesis. While we won't say it is normal, we will say it is common.

A book like this can't solve structural issues, but we can acknowledge them and advocate for more supportive and inclusive systems.

When it comes to some other external factors, here are some strategies for getting unstuck that other PhD students have found helpful:

- Have you been pressured by others into living according to one or more of the PhD myths from Chapter 5 '"No pain, no gain" and other unhelpful myths'? See if you can identify healthier ways of working, even if others in your department don't practice them.
- How is your health or mental health? In 'Self-care is not only for social media influencers' from Chapter 5, we advocate working to prioritise self-care, and working with health professionals as needed.
- Finding it challenging working with your supervisor? Take a look at Chapter 8 and try one of the suggested strategies.
- It's often useful to have somebody to talk to. Think about whether you have a fellow student, mentor, counsellor, family member, or best friend who you can get support from. They don't have to have a PhD or know

a lot about a PhD to be a part of your support network, it may even be helpful to have an outsider view sometimes.
- If what you need is more time, consider whether you can make a variation to your enrolment. Perhaps you could go part-time, take a leave of absence or a formal interruption of studies. Where possible, speak to your supervisor, postgraduate advisor or administrator about how you're feeling and what's possible at your institution.
- Sometimes external factors make you consider permanently leaving the PhD. Chapter 13 'Do you actually want to finish the PhD?' considers some external reasons that make leaving the PhD a valid plan, and how to make the right decision for you.
- If you're an international student worried about your visa, speak to your university's international office. There may even be someone who takes care of PhD students specifically. Find out what contingencies are possible. It can often relieve stress to know what your options are, for example if things don't go to your planned timeline.
- If you have family or care responsibilities, many students choose to go part time, take family/carers leave or a temporary leave of absence. Find out what support is available from your university, but also from your own networks and family.
- Working full-time while studying often makes sense from a professional and financial point of view, but obviously involves a significant time investment in something other than your research and writing. When you add your work commitments into your planning, is your research plan still feasible? If not, what can you

change? See 'Making a schedule' in Chapter 3 for more time planning advice.

We recognize that generic legal or health advice can be dangerous, and institutional rules and supports are so varied around the world. Because this book is a quick overview guide to completing a PhD, we recommend you access resources and professionals that can address your specific circumstances. The exact 'how' will need to be adjusted to enable you to get work done in a system often not built to support you. Many students we talk to who are neurodivergent, have ongoing mental illnesses or physical disabilities, or are carers, are already experts on what works best for them: please use this short chapter as an encouragement to put the strategies in place that are right for you. We'll be cheering you on.

If you are just coming to terms with how the new challenges of the last stage of a PhD interact with your energy, stress-responses, or sleep patterns, we recommend you work with your primary health care provider, and maybe with your university health service, to find out what is best for you. We also recommend you build up a community of other people who share your experiences, either on your campus, or online in communities like the Chronically Academic blog (2016–present).

Reference

Chronically Academic. (2016–present). https://chronicallyacademic.blogspot.com

8 Working with your supervisor

Your relationship with your supervisor evolves over the course of your PhD as you make the transition from student to scholar. But even as you near completion, you'll still need to work with your supervisor in important ways. In this chapter, we look at some of the things you can be proactive about to make the most of the supervisory relationship in the late stage of your candidature. We include suggestions to address any changes that you might need to negotiate or to address problems that may arise.

Knowing your rights and responsibilities

One of the most common challenges we've seen in the late stages of the PhD is confusion about the roles and responsibilities of the student and the supervisor.

The first thing you should do is familiarise yourself with your university's supervision policies. These policies may be available in your PhD student handbook or on your institution's website. If you cannot find them, enquire with the appropriate member of staff in your university. These policies will give you a clear idea of you and your supervisor's formal responsibilities (though you should note that they often provide a base level of expectations and, in reality, there are many supervisors who will offer more support and flexibility). Knowing what the university expects helps you to negotiate the details of your individual relationship with your supervisors.

Most universities will have policy guidelines for:

- The frequency of supervision meetings.
- The division of labour and authority when multiple supervisors are assigned to a single PhD student.
- The role of the supervisory panel or committee, and the formal lines of assistance available.
- Reading thesis drafts – including whether supervisors are expected to read a full draft.
- Assigning authorship fairly where students and their supervisors submit joint publications.
- Administration and signing off on the complete thesis, including who has final say over whether the thesis is ready for submission.

Even if your supervisor is meeting all of their responsibilities, what you need from the supervisory relationship in the final year is different from what you needed when you commenced your degree. It is useful to have a discussion about expectations and commitments, even if you already discussed these questions in your first few sessions. It can help avoid confusion or unneeded stress when the pressure is really on.

If your relationship with your supervisor is positive and productive, it is likely to be relatively easy. Experienced supervisors are expecting there to be a change in roles, and may have already been signalling that they see changes coming up. You can have a straightforward talk about how they foresee the supervisory relationship proceeding over the final stages of the PhD, including expectations around:

- meeting frequency,
- feedback on written work,
- and formalities leading up to submitting your thesis.

If, on the other hand, your relationship with your supervisor is not as positive and productive as you would like, then you might need to approach the conversation with more care. For example, one element of the supervisory relationship we hear students are most concerned about is getting constructive and timely feedback on written work. It's often unclear to both the student and the supervisor what the other is expecting. Sometimes, the student is expecting in-depth constructive feedback, while the supervisor thinks the student only wants to know if they're generally on the right track. At other times, a supervisor is simply noting grammatical or spelling errors, when the student is concerned about the validity or persuasiveness of their data or findings. If you want a different kind of feedback from your supervisor, it's best to ask for it openly.

If the conflict is around the steps or pace for completing the thesis, we recommend creating a project plan towards completion and sharing it with your supervisor as a starting point. We looked at 'Making a project plan' in Chapter 3. A plan is an effective way to demonstrate to your supervisor that you are taking responsibility for your project and are on the path to becoming an independent researcher. It's also helpful as a jumping off point to reach an agreement about how supervision will take place as you near completion, while highlighting any potential bottlenecks or time constraints.

Communicating with your supervisor

Your supervisor might now feel like a close friend, or they may feel like a distant manager. You may have a collegiate relationship with them, or it may be emotionally challenging. You might have very similar communication styles, or communicate in very different ways. It is common to find it awkward to open a conversation about your expectations and needs. But that is not a reason to avoid it.

It can be helpful to use your professional communication skills – or to build up your skills in this area. Professional communication involves:

- Taking the initiative to communicate clearly and concisely what you need from a manager or co-worker in order to complete your mutually agreed tasks (such as finishing your thesis).
- Keeping the focus on the practical side of completing the PhD, not on the interpersonal side of the student–supervisor relationship.
- Having a calm and confident tone that is neither passive nor aggressive. If you are making reasonable, well-informed and practical points, then your delivery should match it.

Not all supervisors communicate in a professional way themselves, but that doesn't mean that professional communication skills won't be useful in those situations.

Assertive communication

Learning to be professionally assertive is crucial to becoming a successful researcher in your own right, as an expert, and a project leader. Assertive communication is the preferred communication style in most Western professional settings. It is not seen as disrespectful or inappropriate. Nonetheless, women and students in many cultures (including Western cultures) are not always encouraged to be assertive in family or social settings, so making the shift to assertive communication is part of becoming a professional colleague of your supervisors, and not their student or friend. (You can see how powerful, but also how necessary, this shift can feel!)

Assertive communication is the opposite of 'passive' communication (Duckworth and Mercer 2006). The passive communicator doesn't take a stand or have an opinion, they just accept what other people think – which in academic writing terms we call 'uncritical'. If they do need to signal difference of opinion, a passive communicator can only suggest disagreement through disengagement, using a 'passive aggressive' style, or fall into whining, 'whinging', or 'complaint' which are often ineffectual (Ahmed 2019; Mewburn 2011).

Assertive communication is also the opposite of 'aggressive' communication. Students who want to be more 'critical' sometimes make the mistake of giving 'criticism' in the generally understood use of the word – to tell someone everything that is wrong about them. In academia, critique is even-handed, and often positive. You can disagree with your supervisor, and tell them so, without needing to apologise for it or be aggressive. Most supervisors will be pleased for you to positively explain why you disagree and what you think you should do instead. This shows them you are taking responsibility for working to become an independent scholar.

Some techniques that can help you communicate assertively and professionally with supervisors include:

- Sending through an agenda for your supervision meetings ahead of time, and then keeping to the agenda.
- Taking responsibility for providing material that will support the kind of discussion you want to have. If you want high level feedback, provide a high-level document, like a plan or outline. If you want detailed feedback on your writing style, submit a small section of text.
- Backing up your requests with evidence: including previous discussions, university policy, academic research into academic writing, or even books like this one.

Assertive communication is clear and straightforward, which helps avoid unnecessary confusion. Many big conflicts can be avoided or solved by proactively talking about the issues (or potential issues). However, it can be helpful to develop your communication skills even further if you have a challenging relationship with your supervisor.

Some 'challenging supervisor' styles and tips for working with them

Many students have no supervisory issues throughout their candidature. This is great, and how it should be. Unfortunately, it is not always the case. Just as we've seen many similarities over the years in how different students deal with the challenges of completing a thesis, we've also seen common threads when it comes to challenging supervisory relationships.

Below we've outlined some common types of 'difficult' or 'challenging' supervisors. Fortunately, most supervisors are well-meaning people, and most 'challenging' supervisor situations arise from lack of communication, mismatched expectations, personality differences, or just the fact that working with other people and doing research are both very complicated and it doesn't always go right.

If you see your own supervisory relationship falling into any of the categories we describe, we've also offered some tips that are often effective, especially in the late stages of candidature.

The absent supervisor: Perhaps their office hours are constantly shifting and it's hard to keep up with when they're on campus and available to speak with you. Maybe they're on research leave every other semester or term. You might schedule meetings with them, only to have them regularly reschedule or cancel (sometimes at the last minute). You might email, call, or drop by their office for weeks or months on end without even an acknowledgement that you exist, let alone being able to set up a time to meet or obtain feedback on your chapter draft.

Possible strategies:

- Create a detailed project plan and share it with your supervisor, using it as a discussion to pinpoint their availability in the months leading up to submitting your thesis. (See 'Making a project plan' in Chapter 3.) Follow up by email with an agreed schedule. This sets agreed expectations.
- Do you have a second or third supervisor? If so, see if you are able to enlist their assistance in your primary supervisor's absence.
- Discuss your concerns confidentially with your graduate administrator and ask for advice on how to proceed. It may be possible to add an additional supervisor. We don't suggest completely changing your supervisor at this late stage unless it's unavoidable (see further Wisker and Robinson 2013).
- Keep a written record of communication, or your attempts to communicate. If things do not improve and you need to get an extension or apply for a new supervisor, it will be much easier if you can provide detailed evidence of a pattern of behaviour.

The micromanaging supervisor: At the other end of the spectrum to the absent supervisor, we find the micromanager. You'll often find this style of supervisor in an organisational environment where offices or workspaces are co-located, such as a laboratory or research institute. You may be constantly interrupted during the day, asked to report daily on your progress, or submit written work weekly.

You may find yourself spending more time on preparing to report to your supervisor than making actual headway in your research. Or you feel you're writing endless pages for the sake of it because you're expected to produce volume at a dictated rate. In some cases, the awareness that your supervisor is constantly hovering over you may undermine your confidence, and make you feel like there's no room for you to be responsible for your own project.

There is a wide spectrum of micromanagers in every industry. Some micromanagers can be reasoned with, to everyone's benefit, and some just cannot. Some have high standards that they want to see you can meet early on, and will progressively loosen their grip when they are confident you won't make avoidable mistakes. Some have had bad experiences with supervisees in the past that fundamentally changed their approach, and now you're unfortunately on the receiving end. Some have powerful instincts to control what goes on in their workplaces, including you, and sadly nothing you can do will disabuse them of that. Sometimes micromanagement is just 'management'.

Possible strategies:

- Spending some time observing your supervisor and how they interact with other supervisees to evaluate whether you *can* change their behaviour toward you, for example by developing a relationship of trust.
- Make a detailed project plan to share with your supervisor, so they can see you are taking active responsibility for managing your PhD. Use it to negotiate when you will submit written work or report on your progress.
- If you're being interrupted when you're trying to write, consider taking yourself away from the office or lab

for blocks of writing time, such as working from home, the library, or a café.
- If your supervisor constantly calls or emails (yes, we've seen this happen), turn off your phone and close your email client while writing. You can respond to them later.

The perfectionist supervisor: This type comes in many forms. Perhaps they are always pushing you to read 'Just One More Article' or do 'Just One More Experiment' before you start to write. Perhaps they refuse to even look at writing that isn't already polished to a high sheen. Perhaps they give detailed feedback on a chapter and insist on seeing it again when you've actioned that feedback, only to give more feedback that doesn't get you any closer to a finished thesis.

Possible strategies:

- Try to give your supervisor a relatively 'clean' draft where minor errors don't distract them from evaluating the work overall. Use tools like your spell checker, and grammar checkers like Grammarly, to pick up simple mistakes. There is more advice in Chapter 11 'Making the words good'.
- Be assertive about when you implement feedback that does not impact the thesis in a significant way. You can come back to word-level polishing when it is most useful to you and your project.
- If you want argument-level advice, submit 'The theoretical structure of the whole thesis' or a 'Reverse outline' (discussed in Chapter 10) rather than a draft.
- Be very specific about the type of feedback you would find most helpful. Examples: 'Is my argument clear

and persuasive?' 'Are you convinced by the evidence I'm using?' 'Am I linking my findings satisfactorily to the literature?'

The friend-colleague supervisor: You're so lucky! You get along really well with your supervisor: you regularly grab coffee together and have lively intellectual conversations, enjoying the synergies between your research areas. Maybe you even dog-sit for them when they're travelling, and they cover your tutorials for you when you get a last-minute conference invitation. That's all well and good.

But at some point, you may find yourself in a situation where your ideas about your work have come into conflict, or you've been waiting a long time for feedback, or you need to say 'no' to helping them out with that research project. The line has blurred so much between supervisor, colleague, and friend, that you have no idea how to approach them.

Possible strategies:

- First up, try just telling them! When you have a close relationship, you might assume they already know what you need. Informing them, or reminding them, about deadlines, challenges, or issues is often a prompt for your awesome supervisor to step up and be accommodating, helpful, or understanding.
- Your friendly supervisor probably has lots of other academic friends too. Just like in a social setting, you can chat to other PhD students to find out if there's an external reason for the situation, or if they have successfully managed a similar challenge with your supervisor themselves.

- Remember that as you progress through your candidature, what you need from your supervisor will change, and what they think you need will change, but not always at the same rate. We suggest you be honest about it. Particularly if they have multiple supervisees, they likely will not know where you are at as intimately as you do, and they can't read your mind. Keep the language on yourself and your changing needs, rather than how they failed to meet them.
- Hold your PhD supervisory meetings in formal work space, like an office on campus. You can specifically discuss your project, keeping it separate from your more social interactions.

The rock-star supervisor: You have so much respect for your supervisor. A leader in their field, they're also really nice. They know 'everyone who is anyone' in your research area, so you know you'll have your pick of examiners and, if you want to apply for a postdoctoral position, having your supervisor's name on your CV or recommendation letter is like gold dust. So many students want to be a part of their research group.

But when you start coming up against challenges, the last thing you want to do is admit to your supervisor that you're struggling, even if, without their help, the problems start to stack up. Your rock star supervisor is always jetting-off to conferences and major meetings, and they have so many other supervisees too, you don't know how you can justify taking up time in their diary.

Possible strategies:

- While there are exceptions, a lot of rock star academics got to where they are because they're good

communicators. Your first move should always be to try to communicate with them!
- Remember, you are not expected to have all the answers at this stage, and your supervisor doesn't expect you to. Speaking to them about any difficulties you've come across is highly unlikely to damage your reputation with them – but avoiding them might cause issues.
- Even rock-star supervisors have a part of their work hours reserved for PhD supervision. You're not asking them for a favour, you're asking to use some of the time their job allocates to supervisory duties. Make sure you know what is reasonable, and then just ask.

The bully supervisor: Anyone who works in universities has heard horror stories of supervisors who behave in toxic ways. The bully supervisor takes many forms. There is the supervisor who pressures their students to sleep with them; the supervisor who plagiarises their students' work; the bigoted supervisor who is insulting and discriminatory to students; the extreme micromanager supervisor; or the supervisor who just enjoys making students cry. If you are facing that situation, then the advice above is unlikely to be useful.

Fortunately, though, many supervisors are not bullies. This means that if you have one bully supervisor, you can often mitigate the situation by getting more supervisors involved in the project. Getting more people on the team is very common, and it is often effective. Getting a co-supervisor to come along with you to meetings, or submitting drafts to a different supervisor to get feedback, can help you to minimise the harm your bully supervisor causes.

Working with your supervisor 103

You might explore making a formal complaint. There are places where it is safe to report bullying and harassment, and places where it is not (Australian Human Rights Commission 2017, Ahmed 2019). In places where a robust process actually supports students, making a complaint not only helps you, but also other potential targets of the bully. See if you can find someone else who has made a complaint and what their experience was like. Your student union, doctoral student association, counselling service, Title IX office in the USA, or campus safety team might also be good sources of information and support if you decide you will take forward a formal complaint. If evidence suggests it is not safe to make a formal complaint, we recommend finding an informal solution. (We hate giving this advice, but your safety is the most important.)

If you feel your physical safety is in danger, please call the emergency services or campus security immediately.

The final option you may need to explore is changing department, university or degree altogether. Usually we would not recommend this option, as it can set your progress back by months or years. You will have to jump through many administrative hoops. Not all programs will give you credit for previous work such as coursework requirements, and many have minimum enrolment periods (typically two years). Your funding or visa might be affected. And starting work again with a new supervisor always involves making changes to the project as they bring their expertise and research interests into the mix. None of these are optimal in the final year of a project. But sometimes, when you can't mitigate a bullying situation, it is the least-bad option.

Overall, you should take steps to protect your emotional, physical, mental, and intellectual health, and work to build professional and productive relationships with people who will be part of your PhD completion support team.

In conclusion: you are an important part of completion

Sometimes we get caught up in the stress of deadlines, the excitement (or boredom) of our research, the challenges of writing, campus politics and everything else, and forget that our bodies, hearts, and minds are also important.

Students who prioritise health, wellbeing, and good relationships may find the final 'crunch' phase challenging, but tend to find it less overwhelming. They can manage. They also find that once the PhD is over they haven't trashed their bodies and social networks, and can move on to their next adventure (see Part IV for more about 'Finishing the PhD').

Now that you have a project plan in place and you are looking after yourself, it's time to get to writing those final drafts and having something you can submit. You know what you are doing, and why you are doing it. The body and mind that sits down at the computer is ready to get to work. The next part of this book is about the words of the thesis document itself.

References

Ahmed, Sara. 2019. "A Complaint Biography." *Biography* 42, no. 3: 514–523.

- Australian Human Rights Commission. 2017. *Change the Course: National Report on Sexual Assault and Sexual Harassment at Australian Universities*. www.humanrights.gov.au/sites/default/files/document/publication/AHRC_2017_ChangeTheCourse_University Report.pdf
- Duckworth, Melanie P. and Victoria Mercer. 2006. "Assertiveness training." in Jane E. Fisher and William O. Donohue (eds), *Practitioner's Guide to Evidence-based Psychotherapy*. 80–92. Boston, MA: Springer.
- Mewburn, Inger. 2011. "Troubling talk: Assembling the PhD candidate." *Studies in Continuing Education* 33, no. 3: 321–332. 10.1080/0158037X.2011.585151.
- Wisker, Gina and Gillian Robinson. 2013. "Doctoral 'orphans': Nurturing and supporting the success of postgraduates who have lost their supervisors." *Higher Education Research & Development* 32, no. 2: 300–313.

Part III
Focusing on the text

In order to complete your PhD, you will need to complete a thesis. You also have to have completed research and analysis, and in some places you may face an oral defence or *viva voce*. But writing the thesis itself is typically the challenge that most students find difficult to conquer. Some of the sub-tasks involved are particular to undertaking a PhD (such as designing an original research methodology), and some have more general uses (such as developing your voice as a writer).

Your supervisor is usually an expert in your discipline and methodology, and they can produce and recognise good academic writing. But they are frequently not an expert in helping you develop as an academic writer. A PhD thesis is a unique genre, unlike any other form of academic writing. For many students and supervisors, their thesis is the only time they will ever write a single-authored, book-length work. If you are finding it tough to write, then that's not surprising! It's hard work.

There are already a lot of excellent books out there about helping you become a better academic writer, as well as advice in style guides, and on blogs like Rachael Cayley's Explorations of Style. We recommend Helen Sword's *Air and Light and Time and Space* (2017); Barbara

Kamler and Pat Thomson's *Helping Doctoral Students Write* (2014) and *Writing for Peer Reviewed Journals* (2013); Robert Boice's *Professors as Writers* (Boice 1990); and Wendy L. Belcher's *Write Your Journal Article in 12 Weeks* (2019). Katherine's last book, *How to Fix Your Academic Writing Trouble* (Mewburn, Firth and Lehmann 2019), spent a whole book talking about how to address your supervisor's feedback on your writing. Peta (Freestone 2017–present) and Katherine (Firth 2012–present) both blog about writing advice, too.

So, instead of trying to cover everything about good doctoral writing, we are going to focus on the writing advice we provide at Thesis Boot Camps, about getting the words down – just getting words on the page into what we often call a 'zero' draft; and then the next two stages to make that zero draft into something you can share with others.

The signal that your PhD is nearly finished is usually a complete final draft of the thesis, so we hope that this part helps you get there!

References

Belcher, Wendy Laura. 2019. *Writing Your Journal Article in Twelve Weeks: A Guide to Academic Publishing Success*. Chicago, IL: University of Chicago Press.

Boice, Robert. 1990. *Professors as Writers: A Self-Help Guide to Productive Writing*. Stillwater, OK: New Forums.

Cayley, Rachael. Explorations of Style blog. https://explorationsofstyle.com.

Firth, Katherine. Research Degree Insiders blog. https://researchinsiders.blog

Freestone, Peta. Dr Peta Freestone website. www.petafreestone.com.

Kamler, Barbara and Pat Thomson. 2014. *Helping Doctoral Students Write: Pedagogies for Supervision*. London: Routledge.

Mewburn, Inger, Katherine Firth, and Shaun Lehmann. 2019. *How to Fix Your Academic Writing Trouble: A Practical Guide*. London: Open University Press.

Sword, Helen. 2017. *Air & Light & Time & Space: How Successful Academics Write*. Cambridge, MA: Harvard University Press.

Thomson, Pat and Barbara Kamler. 2013. *Writing for Peer Reviewed Journals: Strategies for Getting Published*. London: Routledge.

9 Getting words down

Core to completing the PhD, is, obviously, doing a lot of writing. You can teach undergrads, go to conferences, and sit on journal committees – but you can't complete the PhD without the writing. In contrast, you can complete a PhD without teaching, conferences or publishing. So at some point you have to confront the writing.

It's surprising how often students attempt to make progress on their writing by doing everything but putting words on a page. Rather than expecting you to know how to 'just write', we give you some step-by-step advice about producing words, but we also help you to understand the purpose and meaning of academic writing, so you can get into the writing with more confidence.

The writing cycle

What do we actually do when we write? The psychology and neurology of the act of writing is complex, and you don't need to understand it to learn to write effectively and efficiently. But you do need to understand what tasks you are carrying out when you write, and yes, writing is not one task but many. And, as we pointed out in Chapter 3, trying to do everything at once is ineffective.

What's more, writing isn't a single, linear series of actions. It's a **cycle**.

We like to think the writing cycle looks a bit like Figure 9.1.

When we talk about the writing cycle with PhD students at workshops and Thesis Boot Camps, people tell us that this is why they find writing difficult, but they've never seen it visually before.

Let's break down what we mean by each of the stages:

Thinking: 'Thinking' isn't just the thoughts you have before you start typing or pick up your pen. It's reading, planning, and discussing it with colleagues. Developing methodologies, synthesizing materials, and collecting data. All of these things could be classed as thinking, and you've been thinking about your PhD project for a long time by your final year.

Let's use an analogy to help us understand this better. We'll use the example of email – a writing genre

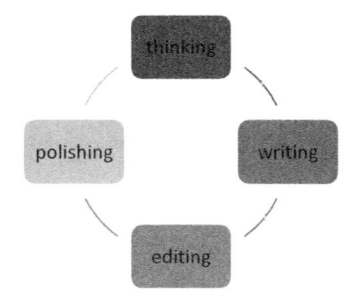

Figure 9.1 Katherine's Writing Cycle (see Mewburn, Firth and Lehmann 2019)

many of us are very familiar with, and that generally provokes fewer of the hang-ups that get between us and our academic writing. Before you write an email responding to a complex request, you need to go back and look at other emails in the thread, double check some details, maybe talk to some other people or look up more information, and think about your answer.

Writing: Writing is when you take what you already *know*, from your research, your analysis, your thinking, and put it into words on a page. Peta likes to say: writing has a sound. Whether it's fingers tapping on keyboard or pen scratching on paper, writing is a kinetic act. It's actually putting down words. New words. And when those words are a first draft, they can be as rough as they need to be.

This is the first draft of the email. Everyone has written a first draft that had all their feelings in it, was way too long, and had multiple spelling mistakes. That's okay, let it sit in your drafts folder for a little bit and you can come back to it later.

Editing: So, you've got a first draft of your chapter or thesis? Editing is where you address the big stuff that needs fixing. Some people call it 'structuring'. Do any sections need rearranging? Are three paragraphs essentially making the same point and need condensing into a single paragraph? Is your argument clear and sustained throughout?

Now it's time to take that email out of your drafts folder and turn it into something more effective. Unimportant or unhelpful information needs to be taken out, and essential points made clear and highlighted. You move that paragraph where you get to the point right up to the start. Everything should be in a logical sequence, and written with the reader in mind. The same is true of your draft.

Polishing: By this stage, your piece of writing will be complete and well-structured. Next you're looking at getting all the details right. Choosing the strongest verb. Making sure there's no spelling errors. Taking care of the formatting. There's a lot of worrying about commas and checking your references. It's line-level work.

This is where you check that your tone is sufficiently formal and polite, that you haven't made any embarrassing spelling mistakes, and that your links are the right ones. You check the recipient's email address is correct, and finesse the subject line.

The thesis is much bigger and more complex than any one email. So what you could complete in a single cycle for a difficult email probably won't be enough for your chapters. This is why we talk about writing as a cycle and not, say, a linear flow chart. With your chapters, and your thesis as a whole, you don't just go around once. After doing a full cycle, you will know what gaps are still there, where more references are needed, or even if more research needs doing and what it must cover. For a typical chapter, we'd be surprised if you didn't go all the way around the cycle three times, and up to 12 cycles wouldn't be unusual. Nonetheless, planning multiple drafts is actually a more effective and productive way of working as we'll explore below.

Beware the perfect sentence vortex

People who try to write one perfect draft have a slower and harder time of it, as we've found time and again when talking to students and academics.

Picture this, you've sat down at your computer. You open up your thesis file and start drafting a new section. Halfway through the first sentence, you've already stopped and deleted what you've written twice. You try changing the verb three times, looking for the exact word to communicate your thoughts. Ten minutes, half an hour, even an hour could go by, and you've barely written a paragraph.

This is a trap that we see students falling into time and again. Katherine dubbed it 'the perfect sentence vortex', and it's something you want to avoid at all costs (2013a). We've established that writing is a cycle, with multiple stages. Essentially, the perfect sentence vortex is what you fall into when you try to do the writing, editing and polishing stages of the writing cycle *simultaneously*.

This leads to writing being a slow, painful process. Every line can feel like it's made of blood, sweat and tears. And what's worse? Your supervisor may give you the feedback that several paragraphs aren't even relevant to your thesis, and those five or ten sentences that you laboured over for a week simply get deleted.

We find that students who write in this way often struggle with perfectionism. They also approach writing as though they are a sculptor carving marble – every chisel stroke needs to be carefully judged, as one wrong cut can ruin the whole block, and then a tonne of expensive stone has to be discarded and all their work is wasted. That's not how writing works. Even the best writers (especially the best writers) do multiple drafts and the writing looks better and better for it.

What's a healthier way to approach getting words on the page than drowning in the perfect sentence vortex? In her wonderful long-running blog on academic writing,

Explorations of Style, Rachael Cayley discusses the importance of accepting **writing as an iterative process** (2011a). Doing this, Rachael argues that seeing writing as iterative makes it easier to understand and accept that writing will rarely be suitable for its intended reader without extensive revision. It may initially seem painful – the last thing you want to do is extensively rewrite all those hard-won words. But really, we think it's freeing.

Embrace the freedom of zero drafts

Give yourself permission to write a first draft that is not as good as a final draft! You can edit to your heart's content after you've written a whole lot of early draft material, but you can't edit a blank page (as Jodi Picoult has said). We repeat: **you cannot edit a blank page**.

So, here are some of our tips for liberated writing:

- This draft is just for you. If you're imagining what your supervisor will say as you write, stop now. You don't show them this draft.
- A simple but helpful trick to turn off the inner censor can be to change the words you use to describe the first draft. Peta likes to call it the 'zero draft', and Katherine cites Anne Lamott in *Bird by Bird* (1995) in calling it the 'shitty first draft'.
- Even if you don't feel 'ready' to write, allowing yourself to write a 'messy' first draft can actually be key to helping you clarify your thinking. You may end up writing and editing more words overall, but you'll be moving towards completing your PhD much more surely than not writing!

There's also a sense of freedom that comes with completing the first full draft of the entire thesis. Work still needs doing, writing the thesis is going to be iterative, remember. But hitting that first full draft milestone is a gamechanger. Peta remembers working with a student who finished their first full draft during a Thesis Boot Camp. With tears of relief, they said 'I feel so much more free. Now it's not about whether I can write enough words for a PhD thesis, it's about which words I choose to tell the story of my research'. We'd agree. (For more on why the first full draft is such an important milestone, see Chapter 1.)

Working it out by writing it out

What is a first draft really? What is its purpose and its function? It may seem odd to be thinking about first drafts, or zero drafts, when you are within the final year of a PhD, but most of the students we see who need advice at this stage still have a lot of writing to do.

We recommend trying to read a really early draft written by someone whose work you respect, such as a supervisor or mentor. Seeing their very, very first attempt to write something will often be a surprising and comforting opportunity. It is easy to compare your initial drafts to your supervisor's published mighty works and despair, but this is not comparing apples with apples. Ask to see the version *they* didn't feel ready to show anyone else.

Until you have *a* version of a written piece, you can't do anything with it. Once it exists, you can start to do something with it. But that necessarily means that when your research ideas finally exist in a readable form, they're not going to match up to the brilliant insights in your head, or in your discourse with your peers at conferences. (This is the 'taste gap' we discussed in 'Perfectionism and procrastination' in Chapter 6.) That's fine.

The purpose of a zero draft is just to get a version of your thoughts for this particular piece on to a page, so that you can begin building on it and iterating what is there. The best way to understand what you think about something is to write a version of it. The process of structuring words and paragraphs on a page – laying out a position on something and why it is important – will clarify it in your mind. That's why you write a zero draft, and that's why it is perfectly acceptable for it to be rough: full of gaps, half-articulated ideas, and repetition. And the parts where you repeat yourself. And also the bits where you say the same thing over and over.

Writing a zero draft will show you exactly where the gaps are: the things you don't know as well yet, the arguments that are weak or mushy. Once you can see those areas, you can target your efforts. You'll have a to-do list specifically for researching and fixing those parts of your chapters, rather than needing to 'do everything'.

The earliest draft is just for you. At Thesis Boot Camps, we often have to repeat this deceptively simple point. You might believe, or have been told, that you must show everything you write to your supervisor as soon as it is written. That is a mistake. You first need a version that is just for you, that you won't hand on to someone else until you are ready. You'll be saving your supervisor time and work too, if you keep a version just for yourself to iterate and rewrite before sending to them for feedback.

So, if you know, deep down, that your first attempt at that next chapter draft is going to yield a bunch of bad writing, do it anyway, and trust yourself that you can do what needs to be done to it before you hand it on.

If you take nothing else from this chapter: when you have writing to do, write with abandon. **No one has to read your writing until you are ready to show them.**

Generative writing

If you're writing the first draft of your thesis, and especially if you've found yourself falling into 'the perfect sentence vortex', we strongly encourage you to try out a technique called 'generative' writing. You may have heard of 'spontaneous' writing or 'stream of consciousness' writing before. Generative writing shares some similarities, in that the goal is to produce words swiftly, letting ideas flow and allowing organic connections to form between them.

But generative writing differs from spontaneous writing in an important way: you first set a goal or plan for the content you're going to generate. Robert Boice describes it as 'working towards useful copy, with some loosely defined goals in mind – but still writing with little concern for perfection' (1990, 58).

Here are some tips to help you maintain momentum and turn off the inner critic while using generative writing to complete your first draft.

One of our favourite tricks to break through avoiding the blank page is to change the genre and mode you are writing in. If you open your document in your word processing software, and it's sitting there looking all very serious and demanding, and the words just aren't coming, try writing in a different mode. For example, you could pretend that you've just come back from a conference where you have met a new colleague who was really interested in your research. Imagine they have just emailed you and said 'hey, that thing you were talking about was interesting, can you expand on that? Can you explain why you did it that way?' If this actually happened, you would likely find it quite straightforward to just write to them, in your own voice, using lots of 'I' and explaining what you did, what you found, why it matters. Similarly, for really sticky sections, Katherine likes to write the first draft by hand. She knows everything will need to be re-written when she comes to type it up, and that reassures her enough to put her arguments and ideas into words on paper.

Try to keep writing even if you aren't sure what to say. Katherine once worked with a student who put a nonsense word in his thesis whenever he knew he would need to go back and write more later. He used the German word for red cabbage, '*Rotkohl*', since German was his first language and his musicology thesis would not be discussing vegetables (Firth 2013b). He knew he could go back later, search for this word, and immediately find where he needed to write more. Peta uses 'blah blah blah'. Students who are not writing their thesis in their first language may find it helps to write down the word in their head, regardless of the language, and come back to translate the individual word later.

You can start to signal your to-do tasks within the zero draft. Many academics use a toolbox of zero draft phrases that they can insert into early drafts. Rather than stopping their writing and going away to do the task immediately, they use these phrases to acknowledge that more work needs to be done and perhaps what that work is. As we point out in 'Making a writing schedule' in Chapter 3, trying to multitask is less efficient than focusing on one task at a time. We encourage you to stick with the zero draft if you are in a writing block of your schedule.

Don't be afraid to write notes to yourself as you go. You often know what work needs to happen to make the next draft better, so leave a note for your future self. If you realise you need to find a reference, you can mark the spot and go back and fill in the details later. Reading/research belongs to the thinking stage, and formatting/fact checking belongs to the polishing stage. You can add information in brackets like:

> [insert quote here, from the big blue Dworkin book, maybe p 200???]
> [explain what I want to say later ?!?!?]
> [XYZ]

Your word processing software probably has a comments function, make judicious use of it. Example comments include: 'I'm not sure if this section is any good', 'Does this paragraph repeat an earlier paragraph?', 'Flesh this idea out on the next draft'.

If you feel a section will need particular attention when you come back to edit it, you can highlight it. Peta does this, as it sets her mind at ease that she won't 'miss anything' later – she can easily see what is going to need the most attention next round.

Getting in the writing zone

When Peta made the leap from managing a university research institute to a self-employed author and consultant back in 2017, she realised she would need to get a lot of writing done under her own steam, with few external structures. There also seemed to be more potential distractions than when she had started her PhD, with the developments in communication technologies and social media. It was time for a writing productivity health check.

One particularly useful concept, Peta found, was Cal Newport's idea of 'deep work' (2016). Newport's main message is powerful: to succeed in their highly competitive industries, knowledge workers – researchers prominent among them – must engage in periods of sustained concentration. Call it 'flow' (Nakamura and Csikszentmihalyi 2014). Call it 'getting in the zone'. Whatever you call it, you've got to go there. Regularly. And you've got to be able to stay there long enough to make meaningful progress. Exactly what a PhD thesis calls for.

How do you find your 'zone' – that magical place of intense concentration where you unpick knotty problems; make breakthroughs; and produce, edit and polish significant amounts of written work? And how do you return there, again and again, without it being a battle? Many of the practices Newport shares could be read as rituals – performative sequences that signal to your body and mind that it's time for some serious work. It served as a reminder to Peta of the rituals she used while balancing full time work and writing up her PhD.

Whether you work from home or the office, there are so many things you can do to not quite sit down to work.

A ritual or habit helps you to get into the place where you are doing the writing, all set up and ready to go, with the minimum of friction. (See Chapters 2 'Getting through the crunch' and 3 'Practical project management' for strategies to avoid procrastination.) Once you've sat down to work, the last thing you want is to fritter away your precious time. But when work gets difficult, when your attention wanders, there are so many temptations your inner procrastination monster will dangle in front of you.

What do concentration rituals involve? Some elements are simple. It could be that you like to grab a cup of coffee in your favourite writing mug, for example. Katherine loads up her diffuser with a scent that signals 'concentration' to her. We'd also argue that there are two underlying principles that make a concentration ritual effective: eliminating temptation and blocking out distraction. Let's look at some ways to make your computer a place of deep work rather than a time-suck device.

Eliminate temptation: Many time-suck temptations are only a mouse click away. During Peta's PhD, she used a web-blocker app to prevent her from accessing distracting websites while she was writing, and she currently uses Freedom. These apps allow you to whitelist websites crucial to your work (for example, the university library) and blacklist the ones that are not relevant to getting the thesis written. Similar apps are available for your phone if you find it is a regular distraction.

Some blockers allow you to set up regularly occurring sessions when you can choose which apps or websites are unavailable, that way you don't have to spend motivational energy on finding the discipline to switch it on. You can also help to signal when it's time to get up from the desk and take a long break, by turning off all browsing at the end of the working day for example.

Block out distraction: For lots of people, music is integral to writing. Back when she was in the write-up phase of her PhD, Peta created a specific thesis-writing playlist. Hitting 'play' on the first track became one of the rituals at the start of any writing session. By the time she had finished her thesis those first strains of the *Elizabeth* movie soundtrack induced an almost Pavlovian response. Wherever she was – café, home, library, or office – her ears heard triumphant strings and her brain kicked into thesis gear. If you've never done it, we recommend giving it a try. Just be aware – you'll probably get sick of whatever you choose by the end of your thesis, so don't ruin one of your Top 5 albums of all time!

If music hasn't worked for you in the past, consider white-noise or noise-blocking headphones. Some people like ambient noises, like café chatter or wind through leaves, offered by websites like MyNoise. Katherine likes to run two YouTube videos at once to get a crackling fire and rain on a tin roof for instant cosy writing vibes. Similarly, you can create custom ambient noise channels with browser extensions like Noisli.

What works best for you will be as individual as you are. Just as your overall priorities in work and life change over time, so can the effectiveness of particular rituals. Sometimes our route to optimum concentration can go stale – even if it worked earlier in our career. If you've found something that works, we recommend putting a reminder in your calendar to review your rituals, perhaps every three months. Think of it as a productivity health-check or giving your concentration-scape a seasonal spruce up. Long term, it will set you up to keep finding your concentration zone quickly and regularly, so you can keep getting those words down.

Shut up and write

Our favourite strategy for eliminating temptation, blocking out distractions and getting some words down is joining a Shut Up and Write (SUAW) group (Thesis Whisperer). In spite of the name, SUAW groups tend to be supportive places. Back in 2012, Peta, Liam and Katherine started a SUAW group at the University of Melbourne on a Wednesday morning. It's still going, and that one hour each week saved our academic writing careers.

The idea of a SUAW group is that writers will get together in a regular time and place with their laptops. One person keeps an eye on the time, and together they write for two or more Pomodoros ('The Pomodoro technique' in Chapter 3). The five-minute breaks can be used for coffee and chat, but after that it's time to **be quiet and get some writing done**.

A supportive group who meets together helps resolve some of the shame that many students will have felt from being told, in effect, not to ask for help but just to 'shut up and write' (Rockquemore 2010). Additionally, the breaks give you a chance to introduce movement and socialisation into your day, sometime often missing for students in the writing up phase – Denise Jones calls this BLAM (Be Loud and Move) (2020).

A regular time and space where you can show up and get some new words written is invaluable. If you can carve out a regular time each week in which you are *only writing*, joining a writing group that meets somewhere outside of your usual workplace or office is an excellent way to nail this part of your weekly schedule. (Remember making a schedule back in Chapter 3 'Practical project management'?) Even if everything else in your week goes wrong – experiments don't work, supervisors go missing in action, IT networks crash – you have at least that one time and place to get some writing done.

There is quite likely a SUAW group at your university or in your hometown or city. You can join in online, we know of virtual SUAW groups on Twitter (such as @SUWTues), on Facebook and on Zoom (Firth et al. 2020; McChesney 2017; O'Dwyer 2015).

If there isn't a group that's convenient for you, it's not hard to start a writing group of your own. Once you find a space, often a café, all you need is a laptop or notebook, and something to keep track of the time. Circulate an email to your colleagues to tell them you plan to meet at a defined location, show up, set your timer, and get to it. We know of many people who start these groups and find plenty of others wanting to join in.

References

Boice, Robert. 1990. *Professors as Writers: A Self-Help Guide to Productive Writing*. Stillwater, OK: New Forums.

Cayley, Rachael. 2011a. "Paragraphs." Explorations of Style blog. https://explorationsofstyle.com/2011/02/16/paragraphs/

Firth, Katherine. 2012–present. Research Degree Insiders blog. https://researchinsiders.blog

Firth, Katherine. 2013a. "The Perfect Sentence Vortex and how to Escape it." Research Degree Insiders blog. https://researchinsiders.blog/2013/03/05/the-perfect-sentence-vortex-and-how-to-escape-it/

Firth, Katherine. 2013b. "Red Cabbage OR [Insert quote here]" Research Degree Insiders blog. https://researchinsiders.blog/2013/04/22/red-cabbage/

Firth, Katherine, Tseen Khoo, Debbie Kinsey, and Hannah James. 2020. "Virtual Shut Up and Write: Now with added Video". Research Degree Insiders blog. https://researchinsiders.blog/2020/03/29/virtual-shut-up-and-write-now-with-added-video/

Freestone, Peta. 2017–present. Dr. Peta Freestone blog. https://www.petafreestone.com/words-on-writing/

Jones, Denise. 2020. "Here's why we need to keep moving!" The RED Alert blog (La Trobe University). http://redalert.blogs.latrobe.edu.au/2020/06/researchers-heres-why-we-need-to-keep.html

Lamott, Anne. 1995. *Bird by Bird: Some Instructions on Writing and Life*. New York: Anchor Books.

McChesney, Katrina. 2017. "Survival and solidarity: Virtual shut up and write, parents' edition." Doctoral Writing SIG blog. https://doctoralwriting.wordpress.com/tag/virtual-shut-up-and-write/

Mewburn, Inger. "Shut Up and Write." The Thesis Whisperer blog. https://thesiswhisperer.com/shut-up-and-write/.

Mewburn, Inger, Katherine Firth, and Shaun Lehmann. 2019. *How to Fix Your Academic Writing Trouble: A Practical Guide*. London: Open University Press.

Nakamura, Jeanne and Mihaly Csikszentmihalyi. 2014 "The concept of flow." in *Flow and the Foundations of Positive Psychology*, 239–263. Dordrecht: Springer.

National Public Radio. 2006 "Jodi Picoult: You Can't Edit a Blank Page." NPR. www.npr.org/templates/story/story.php?storyId=6524058

Newport, Cal. 2016. *Deep Work: Rules for Success in a Distracted World*. New York: Grand Central.

O'Dwyer, Siobhan. 2015. "On the internet, no-one can hear you scream: A guide for virtual Shut Up and Write". Research Whisperer blog. https://researchwhisperer.org/2015/08/18/online-suaw/

Rockquemore, Kerry Ann. 2010. "Shut Up and Write." Support for Summer Writers on the Inside Higher Education blog. https://www.insidehighered.com/advice/2010/06/14/shut-and-write

10 Making the thesis into a coherent work

If you took our advice to produce a rough, messy first draft, you then have to turn that into something ready to hand in for review. Alternatively, you may already have a portfolio of journal articles, or some already finished chapters, but you still have to shape them into what university guidelines across the world call 'a coherent work'. This is the 'edit' step of 'The writing cycle' from Chapter 9. It's a **structural edit**, not a copy edit. We'll look at structural editing here: high level adjustment of the overall arrangement and flow of your ideas. In Chapter 11, below, when we discuss scholarly style, we are going to come back to editing and discuss **stylistic editing**, which is more about a line-by-line revision of your writing.

Editing is complex. We often think of it as a simple, final task, but it actually includes a range of high-level skills. Editing is the process you undertake to make your writing scholarly, and to meet reader expectations. The purpose of editing is:

- first to make sure what is in your head is actually on the page,
- then to get what is on the page to be comprehensible to a reader,

Making the thesis into a coherent work 129

- and then to get it to a state where it can be examined or published.

It can look like a lot, but it's actually easier to edit if you aren't trying to do it all at once.

The structural edit is all about making sure your work contains everything it needs to logically demonstrate your **answer statement** to your **thesis question** (discussed in Chapter 1). There are two ways to go about the next steps to make the whole massive document fit together. The first is **technical**: building a structure that coheres to the regulations and norms of your discipline and university. The second is **theoretical**: how you reflect your argument and philosophy in the structure of your thesis. We'll finish this chapter by explaining some of our favourite practical tools for you to use when structurally editing your own work.

After a few years of working on your PhD, hopefully you have a collection of bits of writing. Maybe you have a number of chapters, or some journal articles. Even if it feels like you don't have anything much, you will have some reports, notes, and drafts. Getting all of it out and putting it together in one document is a massive moment, one in which you realise just how close – or how far away – the final 'thesis' actually is. Usually students are surprised by how much writing they have when they do this exercise.

Putting the thesis together with all the right sections in it is what we are calling a 'compilation' edit. You compile your disparate chapters, drafts and papers into a single document. Then you need to make that document internally coherent. It's a big task to 'bring all the threads together'. Even if you have enough words and they are in the right sections and the sections are in the right order ... you still don't necessarily have a coherent thesis.

Coherence means 'forming a unified whole by being logical and consistent'. It is slightly different from 'cohesion' which means 'forming a unified whole by sticking together'. Basically, coherence is about building an intellectually structurally sound document, and cohesion is about adding in linking words and sections that make the reading experience seamless. You can't paper over massive coherence gaps with cohesion techniques, so you should start here before you move on.

Structural editing

In this section, we will look at three fundamental kinds of structural editing: editing for sequence, editing for inclusion or gaps, and editing for flow. These categories of editing can also help you to discuss which strategies will be most effective for taking on feedback from your supervisor: to get clarification about what they want you to do, or to get strategic advice on what to do first.

These are the processes that work for each of us, and in fact, this book went through all three processes roughly in that order. Editing needs to happen in a sequence to be effective. There's no point worrying about commas if you are going to be deleting the whole section!

Editing for sequence: Your structure is the big picture of the thesis, set out in chapter and section plans. Your structure should be visible from your titles and subheadings. Certain aspects of the sequence are already set by the thesis genre or disciplinary expectations (for example,

Making the thesis into a coherent work 131

we discussed below that in an IMRAD thesis, your methods will come before your results). Other aspects are negotiable, such as which case study to put first, and whether to put all the background information in a single chapter or spread it out across the chapters.

The main question for editing for sequence is: 'does this build my argument?' In other words, evaluate whether your sections and paragraphs are in the best sequence for your reader to understand your argument. You want the sequence and proportion of text to set out the logical flow of information, so that your reader knows what is important and is able to follow the argument forward.

Editing for inclusion or gaps: Once you have the sequence and structure mapped out, you can see where there is too much information or just too many words in some places. You will find other places where there are gaps, or where you have been too concise and need to unpack and explain in more detail.

- The main question for inclusion is: 'What do I have too much of?'
- The main question for gaps is: 'What is missing in my draft that I need to write?'

Editing for flow: Once your sections, paragraphs, and sentences are in place, it's time to make your writing flow. Sometimes 'flow' is called 'cohesion' or 'transitions'. Flow often challenges people, because they try to make it happen before the earlier editing stages are done. If your sequence is wrong, your argument is unclear, or there are lots of gaps in your writing, it is almost impossible to make your writing flow, so it's important to do those steps first. Once your sentences and paragraphs and sections are in the right order, many issues with flow disappear.

If your writing still isn't 'flowing', you might need to try **putting in linking structures**: Do the sections, paragraphs and sentences connect to each other? Linking techniques include bridge sections, linking sentences, linking phrases and linking words.

Bridge sections, like introductions and conclusions, help link parts of the thesis together. That is why you should have introductory sections in every chapter, and sometimes within the chapter, as well as a big Introduction to the thesis as a whole. It's the same for conclusions.

Linking sentences connect paragraphs to one another. Topic sentences can be used as introductions to the paragraph (usual in the UK) or as conclusions to the paragraph (usual in the US). Some paragraphs need a 'link forward' sentence that connects the next paragraph. You should try to avoid too much 'linking back' or cross referencing, but you will almost certainly need to do it some of the time. A linking phrase (part of a sentence) can be sufficient to make the connection: for example: 'As we reported in Chapter 4A', 'See Figure 3 below'.

You can also use phrase patterning in your sentence to create a sense of flow. Rather than start each sentence afresh, try to pick up on the previous sentence in an early phrase, and then point forward to the next sentence in a phrase near the end. In this nonsense thesis example:

> Hamsters are prolific readers. Unlike the reading skills of rats, guinea pigs and chinchillas, hamsters continue to add vocabulary

Making the thesis into a coherent work 133

> at an exponential rate through to the <u>end of their third year</u>. <u>After four years of age</u>, however, they require reading glasses to continue to develop reading skills.

In this example, the underlined words and phrases at the beginning and end of sentences are similar and easily connected, which helps the reader move through the paragraph with a sense that the sentences flow.

Finally, linking can be achieved through individual words, like 'however', 'therefore' or 'finally', to start sentences. These words help connect parts together, or, as we will see later in this chapter with 'Signposting', they can signal when you are changing direction or coming to a stop. Similar to punctuation marks, these words are essential, but you can over-use them and make your writing choppy. Most of the time, you want no more than one major linking term per paragraph.

'And' and 'or' are also linking words, but you will likely find yourself using them more than once per paragraph. However, if you are overusing them, it's often a sign that you are under-using other strategies listed here, or that your argument isn't clear enough yet and you are trying to string it together with linking words!

The main question in editing for flow is: 'Does my writing carry the reader forward, or does the reader have to find their own way?' Hint: the reader should not have to find their own way!

If you are looking at your thesis and you aren't sure how it fits together, you might find a process like the 'Reverse Outline' useful (discussed in detail below).

Regulations and norms for structuring your thesis

It may seem obvious, but when collating a series of chapters and sections into a whole thesis, one of the first things that it is really important to understand is how **long the final document has to be** for it to be accepted for examination at your university. Usually this is measured in word count or number of pages.

A quick survey of universities and disciplines across the world suggested anything from 100 pages ('doubled spaced on A4 paper in normal size type'); '40,000 words and an exhibition of studio work'; '50,000 words and in no cases longer than 75,000 words'; '60,000 words with up to 80,000 with permission'; 250 pages; '80,000–100,000 words' … and the list goes on.

You will need to look at your university's policies or thesis guidelines and talk to your supervisor. Some people will have read all the guidelines way back in their first few months of the project, and have been consistently working towards their goal for years. If you are only just getting around to it, however, you are by no means alone.

You should also be clear on what is included and excluded in the size limit. Administrators will assume you already know (sometimes without telling you) what does or does not count towards your limit. Check what is correct for your thesis, as we've seen different rules for all of the following material:

- Bibliography
- Notes and references

- Tables and diagrams
- Appendices
- Supplementary material that would otherwise be inaccessible
- Source material being edited
- Translations of original languages quoted in the thesis
- Glossary
- Maps and illustrations
- Descriptive catalogues
- Computer output or code.

Once you've clarified what you're required to submit, do a quick count of your thesis, and compare the two. If you already have 75% or more, you should stop writing chapters and start structuring your whole thesis. That 25% deficit might feel like a lot, but you are almost guaranteed to need those extra words for introductions, conclusions, paragraph linking, new research emerging, or extra things that your supervisor helpfully recommends you put into a chapter draft when you think you're finished. (This book went from 41,000 to more than 54,000 between the compilation edit and the signposting edit. We had to cut lots of words in the polishing edit to meet our word limit.)

Thesis 'types'

Next it's time to map out the different parts of your thesis. All theses will have an abstract, an introduction and conclusion, a bibliography and some central sections. However, what these normally look like depends on the kind of PhD you are undertaking.

Start by looking at your university's thesis repository (talk to your librarian if you don't know how to search for it). Your university will have a copy of every successful PhD thesis, and you should select some recent examples from your discipline. Take some notes about what you find:

- What sections do they include?
- How long is a chapter?
- Does everyone structure their thesis the same, or is there variation?
- Do people explain the structure of their thesis, and how do they explain it?

That way, when you make your own decisions they are based on research.

In reviewing what sections of your thesis you actually have compared to what is needed, you need to decide the **'type' of thesis** you are writing. Here, we'll explain the four main 'genres' of PhD thesis and their typical challenges. You might find that none of these are relevant for your specific context, and so we'll discuss those cases at the end of this section.

IMRAD Thesis, for experimental doctorates: If your PhD uses experiments, then it is likely you will use a version of the IMRAD thesis – which stands for Introduction, Methods, Results and Discussion.

For example:

- Introduction: you state your research question, literature review, outline of the thesis.
- Methods: you explain the research method you used in your experiments.

- Results: you will often have multiple results chapters, where you describe your data findings in a mixture of words, tables, figures, graphs, or other materials.
- Discussion: you pull your results together to explain what they mean, and you probably also discuss their limitations and robustness, and the implications for further research.
- You may or may not have a short conclusion.

The IMRAD thesis is designed for 'hard' sciences where you design a research question, make a hypothesis, design experiments, carry them out and collect quantitative data, and then analyse them. It works very well for that kind of thesis, and is therefore often reasonably quick and easy to structure and write.

The structure outlined above also assumes that you only did one kind of experiment. Many people have worked on two or three linked projects, perhaps with different background literature or methods. In that case, you may need to re-organise your chapters, with a mini introduction and methods for the different experiments.

The IMRAD thesis structure is being increasingly used for qualitative and mixed-methods research. For some research projects, especially ones with linear research designs, it can work well. If you are using a recursive project design like grounded theory, this structure can be challenging.

Some academics believe that IMRAD is 'more scholarly' or 'more scientific' than other ways of structuring your thesis. It is not true, but you may need to be prepared to explain why you have chosen a different structure (Mewburn, Firth and Lehmann 2019, 135–6).

The 'Big Book' thesis: In the Arts and Humanities, the traditional thesis structure is a first attempt at a scholarly monograph, the single-authored book that you produce after your PhD for academic jobs and promotion. This means that you will organise your thesis with an introduction, and then a series of linked chapters that build towards your conclusion. You may have an additional literature review chapter, or you might incorporate the literature throughout the whole thesis.

For example:

- Introduction: you normally start with the background context, state your argument and include an outline of the thesis. You will often include your methods, theory, and an overall literature review here – though sometimes one, or more, of these sections is so long it needs to be in a separate chapter.
- Chapters: each chapter will focus on a case study, text, period, theme, or occurrence. It will have some background context and relevant literature. The chapter will be a step in your overall argument, and you will explain how it builds towards the next chapter.
- Conclusion: in the conclusion, you show how the whole thesis built to your final findings, and explain its significance and relevance to future research.

This structure is designed for text-heavy or theoretical research where the argument is unpacked throughout the thesis in relationship to the data, evidence, and analysis. The evidence will often involve quotations from primary and secondary sources, which are then explained in the same chapter or even paragraph.

This structure assumes that your research works as a single and unbroken set of steps. However, if you are working on quite disparate case studies, you may need to re-organise your chapters, with a mini introduction for the different sections.

The 'Big Book' thesis is quite a flexible genre, so it can be challenging to decide which order to put your central chapters in, how long to make a chapter, what to include in the introduction, whether to have a long conclusion or a very short one. For example, a chapter can be anything between 5,000 and 20,000 words, but 7,000–10,000 is most common. There are no right answers, but there will be normal answers in your discipline, so check out what other people have done.

The purpose of a 'Big Book' thesis is to turn it into a monograph. Find some examples of books that started as a thesis (usually an academic's first book), and read the preface, acknowledgements, or author foreword. The author will often talk about how long it takes to make a thesis into a book, what challenges they faced, and how the book changed. You may be able to learn from some of their mistakes! An academic book is usually 70,000 words long, so a shorter thesis will be closer to the book word count. (For more on the 'Big Book' thesis, see Kamler and Thomson 2014, 136).

PhD 'by publication', 'with publications', 'set of scientific papers': With the pressure to start publishing during your PhD increasing, some universities, and some disciplines, now encourage students to include their published papers in the PhD thesis as a chapter. The rules around this are so varied that you *must* check your university guidelines. For example, some universities allow only published papers, others accept submitted papers. The number of papers included also varies widely, Mason and Merga (2018) found a range of 1–12 papers required.

If a PhD with publications is allowed, you will almost always have to write an extra introduction, general discussion and general conclusion, and also to demonstrate that the work constitutes a thematically linked project in some way. Some universities also expect a more extensive literature review and other 'linking' material to give more context and background.

Some universities allow jointly written papers, but then you will need to explain the extent of your contribution, which needs to be significant. Whether or not you are officially the 'first author', you need to have been the major author on the paper so that the article can demonstrate your ability to collect and analyse data, and to write about it critically.

On the one hand, a PhD with publications can be an excellent way to develop your academic track-record ahead of your graduation. By co-authoring with your supervisor, or writing a paper supported by them, you can learn the ropes of how to get things published. An accepted or published peer reviewed article is also highly regarded by doctoral examiners as evidence that your work is already of a high academic standard (Mullins and Kiley 2002).

However, there can be some challenges with PhDs with publication. First of all, some students are not strategic enough about their collaboration on papers, and find their work does not necessarily build up to a coherent body of research, and not enough of the writing, analysis, and argument is done by the student to qualify for a doctorate.

Secondly, getting an article to fit into a thesis can be a challenge. Some experiments are not obviously linked. Sometimes, after a paper has been authored, co-authored, peer reviewed,and revised (perhaps more than once), it has changed so much it doesn't fit any more. You might be able to solve the problem by adding in more 'linking' material, perhaps a page or two explaining or expanding on the paper's relevance to your PhD. You may also include data or analysis that was cut from the final paper (for reasons of space or priority) that you need for the material to make sense in the context of a thesis.

If it's very challenging to fit together your papers, or if the authorship issues are too complex, it may be faster and more effective to write up your research in a more traditional format. It is appropriate to cite your published work. You might also be able to reuse material like methods sections which are impossible to reword, and most of the bibliography. You should include a note that the research was first presented in a publication in the Acknowledgements and in the introduction of the relevant chapter. You may also need to note it in your university's formal submissions paperwork or administrative processes.

'Creative' or 'Practical' work with an 'exegesis' or 'critical commentary': This kind of thesis has been common for many years in creative disciplines, such as visual art, music, and creative writing. An increasing number of other disciplines are now allowing a practical component, particularly in professional doctorates. It is very much an emerging trend, so it is changing quite fast.

In this kind of PhD, the student produces evidence of creative or practical works and also a critical component.

The work might be a portfolio, a large single work, an exhibition or performance. The student then produces either an academic analysis of their own work sometimes called an 'exegesis'; or a dissertation or group of essays on a topic closely related to the work.

The academic written component of the PhD is typically much shorter than for other theses, usually 25–50% of the length. The creative work is often a significant undertaking, such as a whole novel, or composing a full concert including at least one work equivalent to a symphony. Check your university guidelines for how much creative or practical work you need to submit and how it should be submitted.

The major challenge for a 'creative and critical' thesis is that you need to change gears between the artistic/practical side of the work, and the academic/analytical side. For artists who are experts at sculpture or dance, it can be a challenge to go from the studio to sit down and write. For creative writers, it can be difficult to switch skills between fiction and criticism, especially when the criticism is of their own work.

The most helpful thing to stay on track is not to focus for too long on one side of your work. Instead, we recommend regularly allocating time to your creative practice and to the academic side of your work. Regularly reflecting on your creative practice, reading the literature, presenting academic papers, and adding to your critical draft will mean you keep making coherent progress on both sides of the thesis.

Something else: Your thesis might not fit easily into any of these shapes. Go back to the advice at the top of this section and read lots of other theses in your area. Reach out to other universities and read

Making the thesis into a coherent work 143

their theses. You can sometimes order a thesis via interlibrary loan, your national library may have a repository, or your academic network might be willing to share examples.

Just because your thesis is not common enough to be included in the top four types in a general book like this one doesn't mean that there aren't scores, or even thousands, of people facing the same challenges you are. Your thesis might belong to a very specific disciplinary norm that has not been covered here (analytic philosophy, theoretical physics), in which case you probably need guidance from a more specific book. It might be interdisciplinary or multi-modal, and so needs to be a blend or evolution of thesis genres.

Alternatively, your thesis might be designed to disrupt the norms of academic writing, or writing in a language that is not normally used in universities (see for example Archibald, Lee-Morgan and De Santolo (2019) for a survey of recent global research using Indigenous storywork methodologies and minority languages).

Sometimes a student comes to us and suggests inventing their own thesis structure. We are, on the whole, not a fan of this idea – it's a lot more work, and is often confusing for the reader. Your PhD will be original even if you use a completely old-fashioned structure. It is much easier to write in a structure that other people have already invented, and that you can get advice on. Your reader will find it hard enough to get their head around your original research and deep analysis without having to navigate a fancy thesis structure. Mullins and Kiley's research (2002) shows this is true even for experienced examiners!

The theoretical structure of the whole thesis

Having done these technical kinds of structuring tasks, you need to also make sure you are making 'sense', and checking your work is coherent theoretically.

Remember your **central thesis question and answer statement** (from Chapter 1). The challenge is to scaffold everything on this central answer: in the lit review, methodology, findings, analysis, and especially the discussion. It all has to contribute to helping your reader understand your position on your thesis question. Putting all the steps together in a logical order to build your complete answer is how you make your argument.

One technique that the three of us have all found to be helpful, both in our own work and with PhD students, is the 'Tiny Texts' strategy. Tiny Texts is a process developed by our colleagues Pat Thomson and Barbara Kamler. It can be particularly helpful in clarifying what that **central answer** actually is, and why your reader needs to care about it. Essentially it involves asking yourself a series of questions about the thesis as a whole, though it can also be used for individual chapters. (For extensive examples, see Thomson and Kamler 2013, Chapters 3–6; or Mewburn, Firth and Lehmann 2019, 145.)

When chatting with students, we find ourselves riffing slightly on Thomson and Kamler's moves. We ask students:

1. **Situate** – *What have other people said about the problem you are addressing?* Not a literature review,

but a high-level summary of the current thinking about the problem you've identified.
2. **Focus** – *What specifically will your thesis address?* This is the problem identified by your thesis question.
3. **Report** – *What is your data saying about this problem?* What is the research and data you've collected that explains or solves the problem?
4. **Argue** – *What are you saying about this problem?* Yes, this is your answer statement.
5. **Significance** – *What does this add to the field?* Why does your answer to the problem matter? Why is it interesting to other scholars?

First we recommend writing one-sentence answers to each question. These will necessarily be high level and won't capture all of the nuance. Think about how you would summarise if a colleague emailed you, asking any of these questions. What single-sentence answers would you give? It can take time to get right, so don't rush it. It is an exercise that will repay what you put into it later on.

Next, expand each answer into a full paragraph. Do try to avoid making multiple paragraphs per answer. Keep it simple and high level. Again, don't worry if this takes time to get right, it will be worth it.

When you have finished your paragraphs, you should have about one page of words. This is a really excellent abstract, which you can slot into the front matter of your thesis straight away. You also have a clear road-map of your thesis: what area it contributes most towards, the problems it aims to solve, how other people have looked at these problems, how you are solving these problems, and why the reader should care about it. It goes a long way to showing you what the theoretical structure of your thesis should be and how it fits together.

Having a clearer picture in your mind about what your thesis is saying and doing makes it much easier to explain it clearly and concisely to other people. It also helps you to check that your thesis is logically structured and flows.

Logical progression

The word many people use for the PhD dissertation, a 'thesis', is derived from Classical logic. A thesis is a statement or theory that is put forward as a 'premise', that is, an idea or theory on which a statement or action is based (OED Online, 2020). A hypothesis is a kind of thesis – one that you make where the evidence is limited, as a starting point for your investigations. Once you have done that investigation, you have a strong and defensible 'thesis'.

Your thesis should be logically coherent. It should start with established facts (e.g. the lit review) and proceed in clear steps, not leaving out anything essential, to make a reasonable claim that is new knowledge.

There is a surprising amount of variance about what counts as 'logic', or 'evidence' in a discipline, or across national boundaries. This is where you supervisor and department are going to be more useful than a generic book. It is also something to look out for if you are moving disciplines, are writing an interdisciplinary thesis, or are working with an international supervision team.

At this point you may be thinking 'fine, but how do I do that in a PhD thesis?' In order to have a logically coherent thesis, it has to be based on accurate premises. It has to be in a logical order. You can't leave out necessary information. And your conclusions have to be based on your premises.

Logical mistakes will make your thesis incoherent. For example, when you think something is true and it isn't, this will make the rest of your argument collapse. The error can be a slip up, evidence that you don't actually know enough about the topic to understand it properly, or it can be an issue with the state of knowledge as it stands. For example, once Crick, Watson, and Franklin had provided the evidence of the DNA double helix, work based on the previous Levene tetranucleotide hypothesis had to be rethought. As a student writing a PhD thesis, luckily you have a supervisor who will help you catch these kinds of mistakes. If your supervisor says 'you can't argue that' or 'this doesn't make sense', then they are alerting you to a logic problem. Ask them what kind of logical error they think you are making, and that will help you resolve them using the strategies we set out below.

You need to use a logical progression: for example, the order in which things happened, the order that explains why things happened, or an order that goes from the particular to the general. This helps us see how our information is connected and how it leads us to our conclusions. Demonstrate your logical progression is based on sound assumptions by:

- Providing evidence that your premises are correct. Using citations, quotations, transcripts, or data, you can show your facts are true, in a way your reader can double check.

- Providing evidence that you know enough about the topic by including a comprehensive and relevant literature review and relevant background information.
- Using well-recognised theories, methods or methodologies for analysis. If you have developed a novel theory, explain it clearly so others can use it in future.

Assuming your claims are true for everything when they are only true for a specific set of those things can be an error of scope, or it can be caused by not using enough 'hedging' language. Sometimes this thinking is an example of exclusionary structures in academia – it's only relatively recently that Indigenous health, working class economics, women's history or LGBTIQ+ sociology were considered worth studying (Haraway 2018, Chapter 1). In science, it can be seen in the fact that clinical trials often exclude women of childbearing age.

Show your logical progression without over-claiming by:

- Clearly defining the scope of your research, and being specific about what is left out as well as what is included. This is often clarified both in the 'methods' and the 'limitations' sections of experimental research, and is usually discussed in the introduction and conclusion of all research. (See Chapter 1 for more help on setting your scope).
- Using 'hedging language': terms like 'to some extent', 'it may be argued', 'in this example'. You make it clear that your claims are limited, and may not be replicated in other research projects.
- Often we can't see what we can't see! This is why supervisors, peer reviewers, conference questions, and examiner feedback can all help you to know

Making the thesis into a coherent work 149

what you are excluding and how that affects your research.

Logical gaps can show gaps in our knowledge, or gaps in how we show that knowledge to a reader.

Some ways to reduce the gaps in our logical progressions:

- Early drafts are often full of gaps in your knowledge that you know are there. Use the techniques in 'Generative writing' from Chapter 9 to insert information about what to put in later.
- Feedback on your writing like 'unpack', 'how do you know that?' or 'this argument is missing steps' often signals that you have not written down everything that the reader requires to be able to follow your thinking. Things that are obvious to you after months of working on the topic may not be obvious to someone who is reading your thesis for the first time.
- The biggest issue for gaps is, again, things that you don't know that you don't know. Supervisors, peer reviewers, conference questions, and examiner feedback can all help you to be aware of those gaps, so you can go and find out about them.

It is very common to go back at the end of the thesis and do some final, smaller research projects such as running experiments, going back to the archives, reading a few final articles, re-analysing some data, or interviewing further participants. If you are clear about the structure of your thesis, these final bits of research are often quick and simple to write up and fit into the thesis as a whole.

Using these strategies, you can ensure that your thesis is logically coherent in terms of your thinking, and then that you write that thinking down in a coherent way. When you have ordered the thesis in a coherent way, you can write introductions, topic sentences, and conclusions that make that order visible to the reader (see 'Signposting' below).

Consistency

Consistency means that something is done the same way over time, so that it is compatible. Because you are working on a thesis for years, changes in your research can produce inconsistencies in the text. A thesis is typically a very long document, so you can also find that you write about your research in different ways in different places, producing inconsistencies for an examiner who will read the whole thing over a few days.

Do you have the same question all the way through? Do you use the same measures all the way through? Do you make the same argument all the way through? Do you use the same words all the way through? If not the same, are they compatible? How do you justify claiming the whole thing fits together?

Going off on research tangents are an issue for consistency – you should maintain a clear research focus through the text. Challenges that impacted your overall project or you as a person can also provide challenges in your text (see Parts I and II). Radical changes in your research, including changing a supervisor or working on multiple research projects, will often show up as consistency issues in the thesis.

Making the thesis into a coherent work 151

The doctoral journey can often be messy intellectually, personally, and project-wise, and the messiness will all show up in your writing. Fortunately, you can edit your writing. And editing your writing doesn't mean your experience didn't happen. Not everything you learn in a PhD can, or should, end up in the thesis.

Your introduction and conclusion are places where issues of consistency are often uncovered. If you are writing a general Discussion chapter, or you need to explain how various publications relate to each other, you may also find issues with consistency show up in those sections.

Issues to look out for with consistency:

- Your topic changes (even incrementally) over the thesis and earlier chapters don't match later ones.
- Your thesis is by publication and you published as part of other people's projects, but they don't relate in a clear way.
- You are studying something using one measure here, and other measures there, so you can't compare across them all to draw a conclusion.
- You use different words to describe the same thing, so the reader is unsure exactly what you are discussing.

How to fix consistency in your thesis:

- Once you have a full document, restate your research question, methodology, and argument. Something like the 'Tiny Texts' suggested above can be useful here. Note the terms you use, and the scope you ended up with.

- With this clarity of where your research ended up, go back through your earlier work and evaluate how closely it matches. Where there is a gap, you will need to rewrite. You may have to do some light reframing, or use more hedging terms (see above in 'Logical Progression'). If it is too different, you might need to radically rewrite sections, including extra research or analysis.
- Sometimes, it is so difficult to make a section fit into the thesis that it's better to cut it out. You may find another home for that work, for example in a publication or as part of a post-doctoral project. Perhaps the section no longer fits your current research identity, in which case it may need to be deleted all together. It can be very painful to cut sections from a thesis, so we always recommend saving it in a separate file or folder. You will know it was the right decision when the whole thesis suddenly 'comes together' and you recognise the clarity of everything fitting with your answer statement.
- In the conclusion, explain how the whole thesis belongs together.
- Often we recommend rewriting the introduction last, because it's only when you are at this stage that you know how it all works together, in that order, and you can write out your full argument and show how it was carried through the thesis consistently.

We've suggested in the bullet points above that you 'evaluate how closely' later research 'matches' your original plan. Or we told you to 'explain how the whole thesis belongs together'. That is, we know, much easier said than done. Below we give some of our favourite strategies that have helped countless writers.

Reverse outlines

Sometimes it can be hard to see if the components of your PhD do flow logically and consistently. Or perhaps you can see how the whole thesis should fit together but struggle when it comes to moving around sections to fit your shape. A 'reverse outline' can be helpful as a high-level summary to give to a supervisor. But it will be most helpful for you as an editing tool.

What is a 'reverse outline'? You already know how to make an outline plan, listing the sections you are going to write. But that doesn't always translate to the work as it gets written. Your plan may have been over ambitious, or the high-level ideas might not work when you get down to the detail of explaining them. For research where understanding what you need to say is done by writing it down, your plan is only ever a sketch to help you get started. You need to follow the internal logic of the writing, doing the work by grappling with material at the sentence level.

Instead, a reverse outline goes the other way. It takes the work you have already written, and then you create a high-level plan from that. It can help you get an overview of your material, and also help you reorder your writing if it's all in a jumble. Essentially a reverse outline is a document that gives you a high-level view of how balanced, consistent, and coherent the structure of your chapter or thesis is.

All of us have worked with reverse outlines for years. Most Reverse Outline guides help you to structure a single chapter, as with Rachael Cayley's definitive guide in her Explorations of Style blog (2011). But you can also use a reverse outline strategy for the whole thesis (Mewburn, Firth and Lehmann 2019, 86–91).

Steps to create a reverse outline for the whole thesis:

1. Make a copy of your whole thesis in a new document. We'll call this *Reverse Outline Document 1*.
2. Break the thesis down into useful sized 'chunks', a section or subheading no more than 2,000 words or three pages long. Number each 'chunk': do this manually or reordering will be more difficult.
3. Each section should have a descriptive heading. Don't just say 'Methods' say 'Hamsters use magnifying glasses to look at oak leaves'. If it doesn't have a descriptive heading, write or rewrite one.
4. Find or write the topic sentence for the section. A topic sentence is a descriptive sentence explaining what the section contains and how it is relevant to your argument.
5. Save your work! Make a copy of *Reverse Outline Document 1*. Call it *Reverse Outline Document 2*.
6. Delete everything except the chapter titles, headers and the topic sentences. (This is why you need to make copies and save them separately!)
7. Now read through the list of headings and sentences. Do they make sense in order? Do you repeat yourself? Is there anything you have missed? Do you go off on tangents? Do you actually address your central question and answer consistently throughout the thesis?
8. Keeping the original numbering, reorder the sections until they make sense. Add in new headings and sentences for anything that is missing. Strikethrough

anything that needs to go. This is your new structure. (Save your work!)
9. Return to *Reverse Outline Document 1*. Reorder the numbered sections according to your plan. Delete anything that needs to be cut.
10. Add in the headings and topic sentences for sections you still need to write. Write the sections that you have identified as missing.
11. Read through the new document. Does it flow more logically now?

Do keep your document called *Reverse Outline Document 2* because it gives you a high level overview of your thesis as a whole. And you know where you can use that overview? In your introductions and signposting.

Signposting

Once you know where your thesis is going, and the path it took to get there, you use **signposting** to help a reader follow the path. Signposting is where you use certain words or phrases to:

1. Give a reminder of where the reader has already been and tell the reader where they're going next.
2. Communicate what is *not* coming up next.
3. Signal when the argument is about to change direction or stop.

Signposting language works just like road signs as you are driving along a highway. Signposting warns the reader about possible changes coming up, and things to be aware of. It helps the reader feel confident you know what is going on in the journey, and prevents them from getting lost or feeling confused as they try to follow along with your argument.

Imagine your examiners as slightly anxious passengers in the backseat of your thesis car as you drive them to an unknown destination. They know you are a new driver, and that no one has ever gone to your destination before, at least not by this route. They will ask questions like 'are we nearly there yet?', 'why are we making a U-turn?' and 'can I have a break now?' (examiners need to sleep and eat too!). Giving your examiners information upfront means they don't have to keep asking questions, instead they can relax knowing they are in good hands and can start to enjoy the adventure you are taking them on (Firth 2014).

There is no need to over-signpost. If you are driving along a long road (a highway, freeway, motorway, *Autobahn*) with no turns coming up, you can keep it simple with a 'continue straight for 50 km' at the beginning and a warning just before the exit. You don't need to keep interrupting the section with 'continue straight for 45 km', 'continue straight for 40 km' and so on. That would be irritating, and you can save your words for more important things.

How do you signpost in your thesis?

Give an overview of the thesis and say where the reader is going next: In the introduction to the thesis you will have to state the question, theory or argument of the thesis as a whole. Usually it looks something like this:

> <u>This thesis demonstrates that</u> hamsters' preference for Shakespearean sonnets over Petrarchan sonnets <u>is linked to</u> improvements in eyesight. [Obviously a nonsense thesis!]

Making the thesis into a coherent work 157

The underlined phrases are generic signpost markers, and you can use them in your own writing. Phrases like these mean that the reader knows to look out for information about where you are going, or where you have been.

You'll also want to re-situate the reader in the first paragraph or two of each chapter, to help them see where they have come from and where they are going.

> <u>Having demonstrated in chapter 3 that</u> hamsters' speed in reading poetry is improved by giving them glasses, <u>this chapter explores the extent to which</u> hamsters are able to differentiate between types of poetry.

You'll want an almost identical sentence at the end of the chapter, just turned into the past tense, to signpost that the chapter is complete. While it isn't necessarily the most elegant way of writing conclusions, it is very clear. In academic writing, if you have to make a choice, always go for utility over beauty.

Don't hesitate to give us a 'mini-map' any time a complex section is coming up, even if it isn't the place for a full on 'introduction'.

> <u>In this section, I first unpack</u> the theoretical implications of the work of Djungarian and Hamaēstar in *Reading the Rat, Unreading the Rat* (1976). <u>Then I present data to contest</u> their genre-less model of a rodent reader-response criticism. <u>Finally, I propose a new model,</u> which I call 'Cricetinae criticism'. [Also nonsense references. Don't try to look these up.]

Communicate where you *won't* be going: There are lots of paths your thesis could have taken. Perhaps you tried some and they were dead ends. Perhaps someone else has got there first and already published on it. Perhaps you decided it was out of scope. Your examiners will be able to see these potential roads, and will be sitting in the backseat of your thesis asking, 'Why aren't we going that way? It looks much nicer than this road!' Pre-empt their questions with signposts to explain where you aren't going.

To disagree with older scholarship you can write something like:

> While earlier scholars have argued that hamster eyesight was improved by the beta carotene in carrots (Muroid and Glires, 1939; Rattus and Neotoma, 1941), more recent scholarship has demonstrated that this was part of a wider propaganda effort in World War II to promote carrots and hide the use of the new radar technology.
> (Dipodomys and Bandicoota, 1997)

You might need a signpost to show an 'obvious' hypothesis is wrong.

> Although we initially hypothesised that hamsters would have similar reading abilities to chinchillas, new research by Campbell and Roborovski (2021) has demonstrated that chinchillas are confused by all poetry, results we replicated in early experiments.

Making the thesis into a coherent work 159

A signpost is also used to show that research is out of scope, and could be explored by other scholars or by you in future projects.

> The finding that hamsters have literary preferences has wider implications for future research, including explorations of hamster reactions to fiction and memoir.

Signal you are changing direction, or coming to a stop: While the reader is barrelling along your thesis road at 100 miles an hour, perhaps skimming a little bit on their first read-through (Mullins and Kiley 2002), remember to let them know if your thesis is going to change direction or come to a stop. If you've ever been driven by someone who swerved around and slammed on the breaks without warning, you'll know it's a very unpleasant experience.

The usual way to do that is using 'signal' words. A word like 'however' helps us see you are about to turn a corner in your argument. A word like 'therefore' or 'finally' suggests a conclusion is coming up.

Let's go back to our mini-map above and look at it in a bit more detail.

In this section, I first **unpack** the theoretical implications of the work of Djungarian and Hamaēstar in *Reading the Rat, Unreading the Rat* (1976). Then I present data to **contest** their genre-less model of a rodent reader response criticism. Finally, I **propose a new model**, which I call 'Cricetinae criticism'.

There are two kinds of signalling words happening here. There are words that tell the reader what **order** things will happen in: 'first', 'then', 'finally' (they are underlined in the example). The second kind of word tells the reader what **direction** the argument is moving in: whether the argument is moving straight ahead, if it is coming into conflict with the literature, or moving on to new material: 'unpack', 'contest', 'propose a new model' (they are **bold** in the example).

You want to have both kinds of signalling in your thesis. That might feel like a lot, but don't forget that though you are reading over your drafts multiple times, you want your examiner to only read your thesis once or twice over a few days. Students trained in the North American rhetorical tradition have become comfortable doing a lot of signalling. Most other school and undergraduate academic writing styles do not train writers to use enough signals for a thesis that is tens of thousands of words long.

Of course, in writing signposts into the thesis, it becomes much clearer to yourself where you are going! This means a signpost can also be a moment to reflect: 'is this where I want to be going? Is this still the best route to my answer/destination?' Each time you redraft, you can use the signposts to help you improve the structure of your thesis, which in turn will help you explain it in your introduction and conclusions. It might even help you to work out how best to structure your thesis into chapters, or identify sections that you can cut if the thesis is too long. With a really clear structure, you might eventually take some of your explicit signposts out, because the very design of the road is so good that there is no danger of your reader getting lost.

References

Archibald, Jo-Ann, Jenny Lee-Morgan, and Jason De Santolo, eds. 2019. *Decolonizing Research: Indigenous Storywork as Methodology*. London: ZED.

Cayley, Rachael. 2011. 'Reverse Outlines' Explorations of Style blog. https://explorationsofstyle.com/2011/02/09/reverse-outlines/

Firth, Katherine. 2014. 'Effective Signposting'. Research Degree Insiders blog. https://researchinsiders.blog/2014/08/05/effective-signposting/

Haraway, Donna J. 2018. *Modest_Witness@ Second_Millennium: FemaleMan©_Meets_OncoMouse™: Feminism and Technoscience*. 2nd ed. London: Routledge.

Kamler, Barbara and Pat Thomson. 2014. *Helping Doctoral Students Write: Pedagogies for Supervision*. London: Routledge.

La Trobe University, "Graduate Research Examinations Schedule B – Presentation of Theses for Graduate Research Degrees." La Trobe University Policies. https://policies.latrobe.edu.au/download.php?associated=1&id=80

Mason, Shannon and Margaret Merga. 2018. "A Current View of the Thesis by Publication in the Humanities and Social Sciences." *International Journal of Doctoral Studies* 13: 139–154. 10.28945/3983.

Mewburn, Inger, Katherine Firth, and Shaun Lehmann. 2019. *How to Fix Your Academic Writing Trouble: A Practical Guide*. London: Open University Press.

Mullins, Gerry and Margaret Kiley. 2002. "'It's a PhD, not a Nobel Prize': How experienced examiners assess research theses." *Studies in Higher Education* 27, no. 4: 369–386.

OED Online. 2020. "Premise, n." www.oed.com/view/Entry/150302

Thomson, Pat and Barbara Kamler. 2013. *Writing for Peer Reviewed Journals: Strategies for Getting Published*. London: Routledge.

University of Oxford. 2019. 'Appendix A: Excerpts from the Special Regulations of Divisional and Faculty Boards' in 'Notes Of Guidance For Research Examinations (D.Phil., M.Litt., MPhil/MSt in Law, M. Sc. by Research)' (GSO.20a) www.ox.ac.uk/sites/files/oxford/field/field_document/GSO.20a_Sept%202019%20Final.pdf

11 Making the words good

Even when your words are down on the page and in an intellectually coherent structure, you may still have a lot of not-very-good words. You can't hand these words over to your supervisor or send them off to an examiner. This section takes you from not-very-good words to good words in two steps.

First, finding your expert voice is fundamental, so we start there. Stepping into your identity as an expert, even an expert 'in formation' with a very small area of expertise, is essential to writing good words (Kamler and Thomson 2014, 126). Once you have 'found your voice', a whole lot of questions about tone, style, and vocabulary are resolved.

Second, we want you to refine your writing to be more 'scholarly' in style. This includes issues of grammar and vocabulary; style as in 'Style Guide'; and more nebulous concepts of 'what examiners think scholarly work looks like'. These processes for improving your writing make up the 'polishing' stage of the writing cycle (see the 'Writing Cycle' Figure 9.1 in Chapter 9). They are also called 'copy editing', 'style editing', or 'refining'.

Finding your expert voice

If you get feedback that you 'sound like a textbook', or like an undergraduate, then finding your expert voice is going to be important. This will help you move from sounding like a student to sounding like an academic. As we said in Parts I and II, finishing your PhD is about finding your academic identity and leading a project as well as about research tasks.

However, much doctoral writing is wooden, generic, or colourless. It could have been written by anyone. It has no trace of the expertise, excitement, and intellectual connection that we hear when talking to students. Instead, it reads like a textbook, a report, a review, or a multi-authored paper. It's not surprising that the writing sounds like that, since these are pretty common genres that you will have written and read a lot over your academic and professional careers. But a PhD is an authored work, one where an individual has written it, and where you as an individual are being judged. (Eek!)

Your voice isn't necessary in every part of the PhD thesis – the bibliography, and methods and data/results sections are often focused on reporting information in a clear way with little personal style. However, your voice is essential in the introduction and conclusions, as well as the introductions and conclusions of any chapters. Your voice is essential in the discussion sections: whether that forms most of your thesis or just a chapter.

Creative writing guides often suggest you should 'find your voice', as if it is a quasi-spiritual miracle, where your voice 'emerges' or, indeed, is 'found' like it was sitting there all along and you just had to undertake enough of a quest to discover it.

Actually, your voice is something that you already have – you use it every time you speak in an academic context. You have been building it, through decades of learning, thinking, and speaking to others. Your voice will probably have traces of other social dialects in it – where you went to school, the language you did your undergraduate study in, the disciplines you have studied, the jobs you have held, the favourite turn of phrase of your Honours supervisor, of people you read, speak to every day in the lab, and listen to at conferences. You will also have traces of your own 'ideolect' (personal language): the words you choose, the pauses you leave, the way you link ideas together.

The struggle for most people isn't finding their voice, but knowing how to put that voice on the page in a scholarly way. How do you sound like yourself while also being objective and sounding like other scholars in your discipline? Here again, the voice you use when you talk is probably helpful. When we get PhD students to talk about their research, they are usually fascinating and awesome. They are passionate, they are knowledgeable, they know how to convey very high-level expert information, and they can tell when we lack knowledge that they have and are able to explain it to us with clarity.

When you speak about your research, you talk about something you know better than anyone else in the world. The way you talk about your research carries traces of the teaching, learning, and life experiences you have had. And you are talking about your research in order to help another person understand what you have done and why it matters. You will absolutely sound like an expert, because you are conferring expert knowledge.

You will sound critical, thoughtful, and knowledgeable because your thinking and research was critical and thoughtful and knowledgeable. (And if it isn't, no amount of using fancy words will fix it.)

So yes, you do 'just have to find' your academic voice, but it was there already. It was a thing you had made, through your research, and you had already been using it for years.

Here are some techniques to get from your spoken voice to a written voice:

- If your supervisors often say that you talk well about your research but they don't see that reflected on the page, try using that strength: instead of writing a first draft of your introduction, record yourself explaining the upcoming section and why it's important. Listen to yourself speak and type it up.
- If you find the blank screen in your writing software makes you freeze, try writing your first draft in a different space. Some people find handwriting, or writing it out as an email is helpful (see Chapter 9 for more tips on 'Getting words down').
- Whether or not your discipline typically uses personal pronouns in academic writing, write your first draft using 'I' and 'we' where appropriate. This helps you put yourself back in the text. When you edit it out, you will still be in the text to some extent – you will not go back to that wooden, passive writing.

When you speak about your research, you may use colloquial contractions and turns of phrase, or too many personal pronouns. But these are minor stylistic issues. We talk more about that at the end of this section.

Scholarly style and reader expectations

As we said in the previous section, scholarly style is fundamentally produced by scholarly thinking. But there are also a number of steps you will need to go through in order to make sure your expert ideas are clear, polished and presented appropriately to enable the reader to enjoy your scholarly work, and to learn something from it.

Academic writing is a formal genre. It is a high prestige occasion when you officially present your research to experts and senior leaders in your field. You aren't chatting to a friend or making notes to yourself. Formal occasions have rules. They have social norms around how you look, how you act, who speaks and in which order, and some technical terms (see below on jargon) that are likely to be normal in that setting. Learning these formal rules is easier in academia than in many social settings though, because you can lurk in the formal spaces of academic writing and observe the norms ... by reading.

Here are some practical suggestions for how you can use reading to help you develop a scholarly style:

- Download or borrow a couple of recent PhDs from your university. Look at what they do: what chapters do they have? How long is their introduction? What do they write in the Acknowledgements? Are they all the same, or a little bit (or very) different?
- Most people only know APA or Chicago 'style' as rules for formatting citations, but they are much, much, much more extensive than that. Look up these style guides for advice on when to use personal pronouns, how to

format headings, whether to write 'two' or '2', and many other rules. If your supervisor gives you different advice, they will almost always accept that you are following the style guide – something they also have to do when submitting work for publication!
- Different disciplines have different norms, so make sure you are reading books, or getting advice from someone inside your discipline.

However, there is a limit to what norms can tell you about how to write your own project. You are an expert, and you are writing about something novel and original, that extends the borders of knowledge. You may therefore need to extend the borders of writing. This is most likely if you are writing an interdisciplinary, inter-cultural, or epistemological (about the structure of ideas) thesis. You may find that the usual style doesn't support your writing. Or you may need to make a hybrid of styles that fits your hybrid methodology.

Not all advice is good advice. For example, supervisors often say, 'in our discipline, it's not like an English PhD, where fancy writing is a good thing' – but we don't look for fancy writing in English Literature either. You may also have been told that the sciences use shorter sentences, never use personal pronouns and always use the passive voice – none of which is true if you sit down and analyse their articles. These claims are true-ish, but not true. Helen Sword has done extensive research about academic writing styles, and has found, for example, that biologists use personal pronouns (usually 'we' for co-authored papers) about twice as often as historians (2017, 39)! A lot of feedback about the passive voice doesn't understand what the passive voice is. Similarly, grammar pedants who object to the 'singular they' often misunderstand the history and development of the English language (Purdue Online Writing Lab 2020). Many forms of generic advice don't apply in every situation either: for example, 'don't be personal', except you should absolutely be personal in the Acknowledgements; 'Don't use I', except nearly everyone uses 'I' or 'we' in the introductory paragraph where you set out your argument.

Academic writing is the place to be balanced, so it's also important for scholarly style that you don't take things too far. You don't want to be aggressive, or funny. Most of the time, be assertive and measured (see 'Assertive communication' in Chapter 8). When you are confident in your scholarly style, and regularly get feedback that your style is meeting reader expectations, that's when it's sometimes okay to break the rules. You will learn when it is right to give a direct criticism of an idea. Scientists love a good pop-culture pun in the title of journal articles, for example, and so you may learn when it is right to make a joke.

Developing your critical judgement is the most important aspect of writing in a scholarly style, whether it's through the ideas before you start to write, or how you finish off your writing, by editing for style.

Style editing

In Chapter 10, we discussed **structural editing**, the process of moving paragraphs or whole sections around and building in linking sequences so that everything flows. Here, we are going back to editing but are going to delve deeper into **style editing**, where you go line-by-line through your thesis draft.

We'll look here at three types of style editing relevant to preparing a PhD thesis for submission: editing your work into chunks, editing for correctness, and editing for formatting.

Editing your work into chunks: Punctuation, especially full stops and paragraph breaks, mark a break in your writing. Too many breaks will impede flow by creating 'choppy' writing. Not enough breaks will produce confusing and 'rambling' writing. What you are looking for is a balance, and probably some variety.

Think of a paragraph or sentence or section as a step in your argument, to make sure each one matches your logical progression as we suggested in Chapter 10. 'Chunking' or collecting relevant information together can help create a sense of writing that is coherent. Break the sentence or paragraph when you move on to the next step.

Most academic sentences should be 20–45 words long, but occasionally it makes more sense to go longer to keep information together, like in a list sentence. Similarly, paragraphs are usually 200–500 words. However, they are sometimes longer, for example if you include extensive quotations or other evidence. Paragraphs may also be significantly shorter, especially signposting paragraphs, or a paragraph that addresses a topic briefly before moving on. So, make your chunks match their content!

It's also important that your chunking feels balanced across the text. Are there some pages with many new paragraph breaks in them and other pages with paragraphs that run for entire pages within the same chapter?

Editing for correctness (fact checking, spelling, and grammar): At this stage, we are at the kind of editing that a copyeditor does. Most of the time, we argue that writing rules are just guidelines: a matter of negotiation on academic judgement or style. Here, by contrast, you can be right or wrong, and not getting these rules right is a sign of sloppy editing.

Facts must be checked. Quotes must be word for word. Your references must be correct. If you say something is written on page 14, happened in 1812, or weighs 22 g, you need to check that this is accurate.

Spelling is highly regularised in modern English. While there are regional differences, you need to be consistent within the document. For example, in Australia, New Zealand, and South Africa you can choose to spell 'organise' with an 's' or a 'z', but if you have decided to go for the '-ise' form, you need to stick with it.

In the same way, there are grammatical rules that you can just get wrong: such as writing a sentence that doesn't have an active verb; or muddling your subject–verb agreement (e.g. 'I runs' or 'he run' instead of 'I run' and 'he runs').

Using a basic spelling and grammar checker will usually catch most of the common issues. Your word processing software or online checkers like Grammarly will be useful here, though we don't necessarily endorse them for complex grammar yet. Many universities also allow you to get a professional to copy edit your thesis, but talk to your supervisor to find out the regulations where you are.

The main question to ask for correctness: 'Is this detail right?'

Editing for formatting: This is almost the final stage of editing. Formatting includes font, font size, spacing

Making the words good 171

between lines, margins, paragraph breaks, alignment, headings and titles, figures and tables, captions, numbers, dates, punctuation, and what is italicised and made bold.

Your style guide and the university guidelines for submission will give instructions on how to format your thesis correctly. Citation managers like EndNote, Zotero and Mendeley are increasingly effective at formatting citations, but they still can include errors so it's essential to check them manually. Some software like Intelligent Editing is also useful for the simpler tasks in amending style, or you can set up a template in your word processing software. Again, though, you need to manually check your text.

The main question to ask for formatting: 'Does this make my thesis look like a thesis?'

The right words: vocabulary and jargon

The very final kind of editing you should do is to worry about whether you are using the best vocabulary. The reason trying to find the 'right' words is so hard in the first draft is because it is a task that belongs at the very end of the process. Nonetheless, using the right vocabulary is critical to a highly polished and passable thesis.

While we've already talked about using words consistently (in 'Consistency' in Chapter 3), **there are scholarly conventions** around what words can be used in academic writing.

A generic checklist for academic vocabulary might include:

- Remove colloquialisms. You can look words up in a dictionary and check if it has a tag like 'informal', 'slang', 'colloquial', or 'regional'. This book is quite colloquial; our academic writing is much less chatty in style.
- Remove contractions. Replace words like 'don't' and 'can't' with 'do not' or 'cannot'. Again, we use contractions in this book as a deliberate choice – a guidebook is a less formal genre than the thesis.
- Rephrase colloquial or idiomatic phrases: e.g. replace 'is not up to it' with 'is inadequate'.
- Replace metaphors, similes and general adjectives. Anytime you describe something as 'being like' something else, replace with a descriptor that can be quantified or objectively tested, e.g. a number, name, date, or quality.
- While technical terms can be challenging for general readers, they are often well understood by other readers in your field. Where appropriate, use technical terms or 'jargon'.
- If you have written your first draft using the first person ('I' or 'we'), you probably want to reduce the frequency. You can try some simple techniques like replacing 'I' with 'this thesis', or use the passive voice for methods sections where the method is replicable regardless of who did the work.

The main question in editing for scholarly conventions is: 'Does this sound like other academic writing in my discipline?' Reading theses and articles, and talking to

Making the words good 173

your supervisor, will be most helpful here. We don't necessarily advise getting your word-level writing benchmark from scholarly books as we have found there is more lee-way for authors to break the rules in books.

One point that might surprise you is our recommendation that you use jargon. 'Jargon' refers to technical terms that are accessible to insiders (other experts) and inaccessible to outsiders. It's almost impossible to speak or write about a highly specialised and technical area without using a lot of technical terms. Sometimes people use jargon as an insult, but well-used jargon is an effective part of academic writing, as Peseta (2011) has shown.

Technical terms in technical writing, such as a PhD thesis, can be very helpful for accuracy, because many jargon terms have very specific meaning. Jargon can also help to save time, as well-known terms or acronyms often hold a lot of information that are recognised as short-cuts: compare the number of words in the jargon phrase 'iambic pentameter' with the plain language version, 'a line of poetry of ten syllables in the repeating pattern unstressed-stressed'. Not knowing the technical terms makes you an outsider, so understanding jargon and being able to use it will also be an important part of showing you are an 'expert'.

However, there can be issues with using jargon. When you use terms without precisely understanding them, your reader will work out you aren't as expert as you are pretending to be. Because each term has so much embedded insider knowledge, when you use a lot of technical language it can also become very tiring to read.

Readers, examiners, and reviewers may not be experts in exactly the same area, especially if you are working on interdisciplinary projects or in very small fields, so it's likely they will not be familiar with some of the jargon you use every day to talk to your supervisors.

You might not even notice how much you use technical language until you stop and look more closely. To remind yourself how technical your language has already become, try to explain a paragraph or two from your research using simple words. Are your ideas still clear and concise? If so, we suggest you use the new version. Readers appreciate plain language; it is easier to read when you aren't sacrificing accuracy.

Finally, you may have to create new jargon or vocabulary. You may have to name a new species, describe a new phenomenon, or use a common word in an unusual way. New ways of thinking may require new ways of writing about them. But remember you still need to be understood by your audience, so always take the time to explain your new language, and to use it consistently throughout your thesis.

In conclusion: your thesis is ready to submit

After all of this writing and editing, you will have done the work to achieve a scholarly thesis, and you will meet your reader's expectations. If you are not writing enough, there won't be enough to read. And if you are not doing enough editing, you are likely to get feedback that your work doesn't sound or look scholarly.

You can also see now why it may take your supervisor some time to read and give feedback on your drafts if they need to give advice on all of these different levels of writing. That's also why there are so many books on academic style.

Always leave plenty of time for multiple rounds of editing before planning to submit. If fundamental issues are identified in an edit, like a flaw in your argument or large sections that are missing, each draft is likely to take some time for the new thinking, research and writing. However, once you have the argument right, and most of the right sections in the right order, each round of editing takes less time, and gets intellectually easier.

Hopefully, your writing will be getting better with each pass, too, so each time you feel more confident. If your editing makes your writing worse, you may be doing too much of it. Academic writing is not like poetry (which Katherine also publishes). In academic writing, you can't get every word perfect. Instead, it is always a compromise between the new reality your research has uncovered, the technical limitations of style and word count, the norms of your discipline, and what you can express in English. When your readers can confidently follow your description of the complex and original material you are explaining to them, your writing is doing its job, and it's time to hand it in.

References

Kamler, Barbara and Pat Thomson. 2014. *Helping Doctoral Students Write: Pedagogies for Supervision*. London: Routledge.

Peseta, Tai L. 2011. "Professing in the field of academic development: Is content a dirty word?" *International Journal for Academic Development* 16, no. 1: 83–86. 10.1080/1360144X.2011.546241.

Purdue Online Writing Lab. Accessed April 7. 2020. "Gendered Pronouns & Singular 'They'", Purdue OWL. https://owl.purdue.edu/%20owl/general_writing/grammar/pronouns/gendered_pronouns_and_%20singular_they.html

Sword, Helen. 2017. *Air & Light & Time & Space: How Successful Academics Write.* Harvard MA: Harvard University Press.

Part IV
Finishing the PhD

This part is a bit more reflective, looking at some of the bigger questions students ask as they approach their final months as a PhD researcher. Bigger questions such as: 'what does finishing or submitting actually mean?'; 'do you really want to finish your PhD?'; 'how does it feel to finish a PhD?'; and 'what will you do next?'

Of course, there are no right answers about finishing a PhD, no moment when it is clearly completed and your final research is done. There are always more questions to answer and further work that could be done, but not necessarily in your PhD thesis, or as a PhD candidate. A thesis is finished when you and your supervisors agree it is ready to be submitted and your examiners agree it is ready to pass. So there will need to be personal reflection and negotiation.

12 Reflecting on what it means to be a researcher

'When do you think you'll submit?' is a query that applies equally to someone on the way to finishing a PhD and someone forced to yield to a powerful opponent. The thesaurus offers equivalents like 'succumb, acquiesce, surrender', as well as 'propose, offer, put forward'. The phrases that we use to describe critical milestones in a doctoral student's journey reveal a great deal about the meanings we give to these moments.

What does it really mean to 'submit', and the state of being known as 'submitted'? When we say 'I've submitted', those working within or close to doctoral education hear that a person has finished their thesis and handed it in for examination. They have submitted their work for review. But they are also submitting *themselves* to assessment, a judgement of whether or not the submitter can be recognised as a peer scholar.

When we say a person has 'completed' or is 'a few months away from completion' we invoke similar things. We are talking about the work itself, of course, the project a student has been working on for three-plus years. But as the person 'completing' the work, it is easy to think of it as a process of 'completing' yourself. The language implies you are on the verge of becoming a whole person – but you are already whole.

To think of the end of a PhD as a process of completing and submitting yourself is fraught with problems. You are finishing one milestone of your academic and professional life. It is an area of practice, but an area that can become so all-consuming that it is easy to consider it your whole life and your whole self. But **you are not your thesis**.

Knowledge beyond the thesis

Higher education is (in theory) where we develop the tools for, and appreciation of, lifelong learning. With responsibility to finish a project the size and complexity of a PhD thesis, it is easy to fall into thinking that you are completing the final word on your topic and that what you gain from it will be the knowledge and the arguments in the thesis itself.

However, your thesis contains only one type of knowledge, and not necessarily the one that will help you most, or the one for which people are going to want to hire you in the future. Aristotle said there are three types of knowing: *techne*, *episteme*, and *phronesis*. *Techne* can roughly be described as 'know how': having the required understanding to replicate and deploy a skill. *Episteme* is to have a strong theoretical knowledge. *Phronesis* was, for Aristotle, the 'best' kind of knowledge to have: knowledge that was based on lived experience, and more importantly, experience that has been reflected on. Not just knowing how to do a thing, not just knowing why the thing works, but doing the thing and then critically reflecting on why the thing worked, what about it did not work, and what you would do differently the next time you have to do the thing.

Keith Grint has translated the word '*phronesis*' as 'practical wisdom' (2007, 233), wisdom that is 'learned from experience', ideally your own. This type of learning is necessarily always an 'unfinished' process. You can never stop learning from experience. You can always find ways to improve upon your practice in future. Most higher education institutions will include the ability to become a reflective practitioner among their idealised graduate attributes. It is one of the most critical things that you will take from finishing a PhD. Groopman explains the use of *heuristics* (a sufficient and practical problem solving technique) in his famous *How Doctors Think* (2007). Heuristics are learned through experience and subsequent reflection on why and how a diagnosis was wrong previously. While medical students learn medical theory and gain hands-on instruction through placements at university, they only develop their true skill as doctors when they have had the chance to gain that type of insight that Aristotle would call *phronesis*.

As every day of the last year of a PhD is almost inevitably thesis, thesis, thesis, it can feel like there is not enough time or space to dig deeper into all the other knowledge and skills that are *not* just the research itself. However, it is crucial you do reflect. When you do leave the thesis experience behind, it is all that other 'stuff' that people are going to be most interested in: your ability as a critically reflective practitioner to take the skills you gained during the PhD and apply them to new, multidisciplinary, and difficult problems that might have nothing at all to do with your thesis research (as we also said in Chapter 4, 'Working with your strengths and weaknesses').

The key is to know what you can do that's not only the content of your research, but is about you as a whole person, thinker, and actor. And that individual, we are convinced, will never be 'completed' or 'submitted'. You are not your thesis, but, in some way, the thesis will always be a part of you.

References

Grint, Keith. 2007. "Learning to lead: Can Aristotle help us find the road to wisdom?" *Leadership* 3, no. 2: 233. 10.1177/1742715007076215.

Groopman, Jerome. 2008. *How Doctors Think*. Boston, MA: Houghton Mifflin Harcourt.

13 Do you actually want to finish the PhD?

Thinking that your thesis 'will always be a part of you' can be a horrific thought if you are not enjoying the experience, and if you regularly think about quitting. Students experiencing feelings of being 'stuck' may find themselves asking the dreaded question: 'should I quit my PhD?' Understanding the reasons why you feel 'stuck' will help you move forward, regardless of whether your ultimate choice is to complete the PhD or to set off in a new direction.

Out of the thousands of students we've worked with around the world, most are able to find the support they need to help them continue with their studies and progress toward graduation. But that's not always the case. And that's *okay*. No, your eyes are not deceiving you. In a book about finishing a PhD, we are saying that we wholeheartedly believe that sometimes choosing to exit the PhD is the healthiest and most appropriate option. In fact, Peta thought seriously about leaving her PhD a number of times, almost walking away in the final year. So we write this understanding your experience from the inside.

To explain, let's take a look at some student experiences.

Steve: Steve graduated his undergraduate engineering degree with honours and immediately secured a job in industry. He enjoys his work, and his salary improves nicely with each annual review. Then, management changes make his job simultaneously more stressful and less fulfilling. Steve is still in contact with friends from university. A few are studying PhDs. When Steve complains about his work situation, they encourage him to make a change. 'Do a PhD,' they told him, 'we find it really satisfying.'

Steve enrols in a PhD, taking a big pay cut to go part time at his job. A year later, he passes his first PhD committee hurdle. Most people would be pleased. But, at home, Steve is the main breadwinner, and his family are now under financial stress. Meanwhile he isn't gaining the intrinsic enjoyment from his PhD project that his friends experienced. He finds the theoretical components mind-numbingly boring. He realises he's miserable.

After careful consideration, several honest discussions with his supervisory team and his employer, Steve withdraws from his PhD and goes back to work fulltime. Several years later, Steve is a senior manager at a new company. He is responsible for a team he's assembled himself, working on projects that bring him satisfaction with their defined and tangible outcomes. What's more, he's enjoying a wage that gives his family a comfortable lifestyle. When asked if he regrets walking away from his PhD, Steve laughs, 'It's one of the best choices I ever made.'

Anjali: A poet and essayist, Anjali has won awards for her writing and activism. When she moves to the US for her PhD, she cobbles together her income from partial funding from a diversity scheme, performing her poetry at spoken-word gigs, teaching community workshops, freelance editing, tutoring during term, and working one day per week in the student administration centre at another university across the city. Spread across so many commitments, it's difficult for Anjali to carve out time for her creative PhD – her first novel and the accompanying critical thesis on the experience of young women in the South Asian diaspora. Though she often feels stretched, Anjali mostly enjoys the PhD experience. Then her supportive supervisor takes a promotion at another university.

Anjali finds herself at sea. Nobody else in her department (including her replacement supervisor) understands her field, and her repeated requests for feedback or assistance to develop her critical thesis yield little results. Soon, her replacement supervisor begins avoiding her, and when she seeks help to deal with this, the only option she's presented with is to lodge a formal grievance to the dean. Around the same time, Anjali's grandmother back in India falls ill. Anjali loses sleep through worry. Struggling to keep up with her freelance schedule, she has no time to see friends. She spends less and less time on her thesis, falling further behind.

She decides to take an intermission of studies for six months. She spends that time at home with her grandmother, and begins to feel more herself. Dread pools in the pit of her stomach when she thinks of returning to her university. Her grandmother encourages her to listen to her heart. Anjali makes the difficult decision to withdraw from her PhD.

In the subsequent years, Anjali travels, writes, performs, and works in activism for several NGOs, publishing several papers in practitioner journals. Almost a decade later, Anjali still thinks about what could have been if she had completed her thesis. She begins to investigate her options, and returns to study, completing a PhD on a very similar topic to the one she started, but at a university with depth of support in her research area, and with full funding. She happily completes, and goes on to become a full time academic lecturer, supervising students of her own.

Róisín: For Róisín, it's a dream come true when she gains entry to a politics PhD programme. She thrives on university life – joining committees, getting elected as vice president of the student body, attending demonstrations and organising fundraisers. She gets along brilliantly with both her supervisors, tutors undergraduate courses, and even coordinates a Master's unit on policy studies. Her committee signs off on her annual reports, and she progresses through her candidature as planned.

But in the fourth year, Róisín still hasn't made significant progress on the actual thesis. She gets a warning from her committee about timely completion and switches to part-time enrolment to give herself time to catch up. No longer embedded in university life, she pursues employment and other interests off campus. Two years later, her formal candidature is technically due to lapse, but she convinces her committee to give her an extension. For the next few weeks, she makes an effort to get thesis words down, but, no longer fuelled by being part of a scholarly community, her enthusiasm wanes. Still, she isn't a 'quitter'. She can't let it go.

Three years later, it's the last straw. Róisín either needs to hand in her thesis, or the university will discontinue her candidature. She takes a good look at her life.

It's very different from when she started. Her priorities have shifted, and she no longer dreams of employment in her PhD area. The scholarly debate on her thesis topic has moved on in the intervening years, and she would need to do significantly more research to hand in an acceptable PhD thesis. Still on good terms with her supervisors, Róisín has a frank discussion with them. They agree she will collate the writing she has already done from conference papers and annual reports into a shorter thesis. She does this, and exits with a Master's by Research. Róisín leaves campus for the final time breathing a huge sigh of relief, and never looks back.

We can see from Róisín, Anjali, and Steve's story that there are a variety of reasons to quit a PhD. Finances, family care responsibilities, or living away from loved ones. You might lose interest or realise with hindsight that a PhD isn't the right path for you. Your university may have let you down. Perhaps things just really haven't worked out in your research, and it's better to give yourself the closure of discontinuing so that you can get on with the good things in life.

Moving towards a decision

The very nature of a PhD – multiple years of challenging study – means many people will wonder, at one point or another, whether it's worth the effort. That's nothing to feel shame about. In fact, considering all the options is a healthy, sensible thing to do in any circumstances. We'd encourage you to explore those thoughts, rather than gritting your teeth and shoving them aside.

188 *Finishing the PhD*

If you'd like some help thinking through your many options before coming to a decision, you can try some of the strategies below:

- **Thesis Boot Camp**: There's a reason we list TBC as the first option: we've seen time and again how this three-day intensive writing programme for late stage PhD students has helped them turn their thesis around. Some people come into Thesis Boot Camp on the verge of quitting. Most leave feeling confident, empowered, and motivated.
- **SWOT Analysis**: Identify your 'Strengths, Weaknesses, Opportunities, and Threats'. SWOT analysis is a technique you may associate with organisations rather than individual decision-making, but it can be a very useful tool. Think of it as a directed 'pros and cons' list.
- **Read over your research or writing journals**: One of the reasons we suggest keeping research and writing journals is that you often know the best answer and your past-self has written it down (see Chapters 3 and 4). Reading over the journal can help you realise how you have been feeling over a long period of time.
- **Supervisors**: If your supervisors have demonstrated they are supportive, it can be helpful to talk about your thoughts with them. If they are encouraging, that might be the help you need to stay. Or they may recognise that you are ready to move on and can talk through options so you do that in the best way for you.
- **Doctoral Support Staff**: There are likely to be staff at your university whose job is to provide auxiliary support for doctoral students (we find people in these roles are generally sympathetic and solution driven).

Even if it is simply to find out the administrative options open to you, it's worth having a chat with them sooner rather than later.
- **Friends and family**: Can you ask for more support? Perhaps a little help with childcare, finances, or household chores would make all the difference to whether it feels like you can keep going with your studies.
- **Counselling**: If you are able to access counselling on campus or off, it can help as part of the decision-making process. You do not need to have any other mental health challenges or 'major' life events taking place. Rather, deciding to discontinue a PhD is a major life event in itself, often tied up in your identity. Speaking to a professionally trained and impartial person can help you clarify how you wish to proceed.
- **Taking a formal break**: Whether your university calls it a 'leave of absence', 'intermission from studies' or something else, a formal break stops the clock ticking on your candidature, allowing you to rest or deal with extenuating circumstances in your life without 'PhD guilt'. A formal period away can offer clarity on why you would choose to stay or go, giving you the confidence and energy to proceed either way.

Consider all your options, and then decide the best thing for you. Walking away from a PhD can be a healthy decision that doesn't make the sky fall or 'ruin your life', even if it may seem like a doom-laden prospect at the time.

On the other hand, asking whether you should walk away can be a powerful tool to find out that you actually do want to continue. Reconnecting with why you're doing a PhD will help you meet the challenges along the road to completion, or to whatever else happens once you finish your PhD studies.

What's more, whether you decide to finish the PhD by submitting a completed thesis, or by walking away, the skills, ideas, and insights you gained during the process will always be yours.

14 Relief and grief of finishing a PhD

People often say, 'I hate writing; I love having written' (apocryphally, originally Dorothy Parker; Slotnik 2016). But one thing we don't always talk about, is that having completed a PhD is also tough. Personally, we all found the immediate aftermath of having written a PhD wasn't as initially fun as we were expecting.

Successfully completing a PhD is such a major identity change that we recognise it with a new title – Doctor. As with any significant identity change or life event, there are some significant emotions involved too. In this chapter we'll talk about what's great about having completed, and also what's hard about having completed. Let's start with the hard stuff!

What's tough about having finished a PhD

When a major project comes to an end, it's common to experience a period of feeling low. You will probably be tired after all that work. But you will also start to miss the team, the project, and the excitement of research. In theatre, this is called 'post-show blues'. We recognise that after the camaraderie, bright lights, applause, and culmination of all our hard work, we are back in the ordinary world. It's normal and healthy to feel a bit 'post-show blues' about the end of a PhD.

Your office mates, campus friends and your supervisor may have become important members of your life. If you don't have an ongoing teaching or research contract with the same university, you might not be around on campus much after you have submitted your thesis. If they have been positive parts of your life, it is good to acknowledge that you will miss them!

At the end of the PhD, people often move cities or countries. You might be relocating to start a new job, or your visa may have come to an end. Perhaps the end of the PhD is a chance to go travelling or start a family. These are life choices that focus away from academia, or from your PhD institution. Even if that change is only temporary, or even if you are, on balance, mostly delighted with the change – recognising the change, and acknowledging it involves some losses, is a good idea.

For some people, finishing the PhD means saying farewell to being a researcher. If you had dreams of going on to have a research career that probably aren't going to work out, then there is grief at knowing that next dream won't come true. Graduating can mean losing your library borrowing rights, your institutional affiliation, or access to research materials and communities. Katherine often says if she were doing her PhD again, she wouldn't have bothered submitting her thesis in three years exactly, but would have taken an extra six months of library access and student discounts to get an article published.

The first years out from the PhD can be a further period of uncertainty and stress. We know: we've all been there. It might mean applying for lots of jobs (and not getting most of them). It might involve short-term or casual contracts. You might not be earning much straight out of the PhD, and bills, debts, and student loans might be hanging over you. Access to student funding, health care, or accommodation might have been important to your wellbeing for the last few years, and losing those support structures might make things extremely challenging as the PhD comes to an end.

Emotions acknowledging loss are part of a multifaceted set of feelings we call 'grief' (Stix 2011). Grief might mean you feel sadness, but you might also feel angry, blank, or depressed. Grieving also includes feelings like relief, laughter, or celebration. Expect to have lots of different and even contradictory feelings, and know that these emotions vary in intensity for different people. If you were not very emotionally or personally invested in your PhD, or if not much changes in your life at the end of the PhD, then you might not have particularly strong emotions about it.

Whatever you feel or don't feel is normal and fine! Don't feel you need to suppress your feelings, even if they are 'ugly' or seem inappropriate to the people around you. Suppressing your feelings is a major factor in reactive depression and trauma, so appropriately acknowledging how you feel is probably a better idea.

Your cultural background might give you well-defined ways to acknowledge loss, which may feel appropriate to use here. Our academic culture normally expects that you will give ritual gifts of gratitude to your supervisors. Depending on your local norms, the gifts can range from a card and a small token, like flowers, a box of chocolates or bottle of wine; up to quite expensive and valuable presents. You will often have a social event for friends and colleagues, like a dinner, or meeting up at a pub. Graduation itself, with its formal language and special robes, is also designed to be a ritual that marks the transition from student to graduate. It can be a very cathartic and meaningful ritual to go to a graduation ceremony if you have been motivated throughout your PhD by the idea of the 'floppy hat', or the image of walking across the stage to receive your testamur from the Chancellor as your family claps. If you graduate *in absentia*, like Peta and Katherine both did because they were living overseas, you may want to create your own ritual, something to demarcate between student and doctor.

Recognising that this stage has finished and that you will be moving on and leaving some things behind is important. This is also an important moment for thanking those who helped you along the way.

What's easy about having finished a PhD

When Katherine was doing her PhD, she read a short story by Sheridan Le Fanu, one of the masters of nineteenth-century horror fiction. In it, a character stays up too late studying a mysterious text, only to be haunted by a monkey demon who seems to follow him everywhere, to bed, in church, on a bus journey ... until he died of fright.

For Katherine, and when she told the story to Peta, this story resonated with their feeling of the 'PhD guilt' that we carried all the way through the PhD. That lurking presence that muttered 'you should be writing' in the back of our minds, even when we were taking a well-earned break, or trying to get enough sleep. Naming the monkey helped us to manage the feeling that we couldn't escape our PhD (Firth 2015). You may feel the same.

The wonderful news is that when you hand in the PhD, the demon monkey of PhD guilt disappears. It might take a week or two, but you will soon realise that you can sit down to read a novel or watch TV and there is no nagging sense that you should be working on your thesis. You go out with friends, do your day job, hang out with your family, pick up your hobbies, and you don't feel so torn. Even if you stay in research, later research projects are more likely to be collaborations – and it's emotionally and intellectually easier to work in a team (when it's a highly functioning team!), and later academic writing projects are much easier when you know what you are doing.

Your next steps are also likely to be an exciting chance to develop your career. It may take years to get there, but having a PhD typically enables you to do more rewarding work, and to earn a (slightly) higher salary, than you would have without a PhD (e.g. QILT 2019). Your PhD might enable you to get involved in side-projects, such as giving some guest lectures, developing consulting expertise, or being part of other research.

And finally, there is a huge relief in successfully completing a major project. You set out to take up a massive challenge, you persevered, solved lots of problems, learned lots of new things, and now you know you can do it because you did it. Well done!

Other challenges between completing the thesis and finishing a PhD

Some doctoral systems, typically in Europe, have an oral defence or '*viva voce*' as the final hurdle before completing your PhD. If this is likely to be your experience, we recommend Murray's *How to Survive Your Viva* (2009). If you are completing a thesis with practical or creative elements, or a thesis with publications, these will also need to be completed. This is beyond the scope of this short book, but we recommend other books in this series like Salmons and Kara, *Publishing from your Doctoral Research* (2019).

In conclusion: where next?

Whatever you do next, make sure to take a moment to celebrate your achievement in finishing the PhD. However it got finished, mark that moment. Also, give yourself a chance to rest and recuperate.

There are as many paths beyond the PhD as there are people who do them. People return to their old jobs and they take up new roles. People move across the country or the world, or they stay in the same place. They continue on in the university, they move to other research roles, or they do something quite different.

You may take a step into your long-term career trajectory, or piece together a portfolio of short-term roles. If you are planning to move industries, that is likely to require further training and work experience. It's quite common to take a few years to really establish into your 'next', but while that's happening you still need to pay bills and get on with life. That is often a challenge, but it helps if you've planned and prepared for it.

When you are making plans, do your research. Start to check out what kinds of jobs are offered, how many there are, where they are based, what their salaries are. Talk to recent graduates to see how they are getting on. Information about the state of the job market is easily available if you look for it. Senior academics often give advice based on their experiences, but the entire labour market has changed radically in the last few decades, so it's important to use up-to-date information when making decisions.

For the three of us, while we each use elements of our PhD expertise in our current roles, the way we use them would probably be a surprise to our past student-selves. In addition to the work we do helping students around the world, in running workshops and mentoring writers, we use our PhDs in a variety of applications. Katherine uses her work on institutional collaboration as a manager; Liam uses his experience of being a researcher to develop research education and development programs; and Peta uses her knowledge about the spread of diseases to construct fiction plots. We all used our knowledge about what works in getting a thesis finished to finish this book.

Your own post-PhD journey might also take you to unexpected places. We think that's part of what is so awesome about becoming a scholar. We hope you do, too.

References

Firth, Katherine. 2015. "The Monkey Demon of PhD Guilt." Research Degree Insiders blog. https://researchinsiders.blog/2015/12/28/the-monkey-demon-of-phd-guilt/.

Le Fanu, J. Sheridan. 1872. 2018. "Green tea." in *A Glass Darkly*. Peterborough, Ontario: Broadview Press.

Murray, Rowena. 2009. *How to Survive Your Viva: Defending a Thesis in an Oral Examination: Defending a Thesis in an Oral Examination*. London: McGraw-Hill Education.

QILT. 2019. 'Graduate outcomes survey." Quality Indicators for Learning and Teaching (Australia). www.qilt.edu.au/qilt-surveys/graduate-employment.

Salmons, Janet and Helen Kara. 2019. *Publishing from Your Doctoral Research: Create and Use a Publication Strategy*. London: Routledge.

Slotnik, Daniel E. 2016. "The Eternally quotable Dorothy Parker." *The New York Times*. June 7. http://nyti.ms/2bGvBly.

Stix, Gary. 2011. "The neuroscience of true grit." *Scientific American* 304, no. 3: 28–33. 10.2307/26002433.

Index

absent supervisors 96–97
abstracts 145
academic achievement 81–82
activists 50–51
aggressive communication 94–95
answer statements 16–18, 19, 129, 144, 145, 152
anxiety 60, 66
apps 41, 67, 123–124
arguments 11–12; answer statement 16–17; editing 131, 175; signposting 155–156; supporting material 22
Aristotle 180, 181
assertive communication 94–95, 99, 168
attrition 3
authorship 91, 140, 141

Belcher, Wendy L. 108
beliefs 73, 86
bibliographies 134, 141, 163
'Big Book' theses 138–139
big picture 17
blogs 45, 89, 107
Boice, Robert 108, 119
breaks: apps 123–124; ergonomics 63; formal 189; holidays 61–62; Pomodoro technique 39–41
brick wall, hitting a 54
bridge sections 132
bullying 75, 102–104
burnout 61, 62

calendars 35
Cayley, Rachael 107, 115–116, 153
challenging supervisor styles 95, 96–104
chapters 44, 131, 138, 139
Chronically Academic blog 89
chunking 154, 169
Cirillo, Francesco 39–40
citations 141, 147, 166, 171
co-authorship 140
co-supervisors 102
coherence 128–160, 169
cohesion 130, 131–132
colloquialisms 172
communication 93–95, 97, 101–102
complaints against supervisors 103
completion 179–180, 195–196
concentration 64, 65, 122, 123, 124–125

conclusions: 'Big Book' theses 138; bridge sections 132; consistency 151, 152; IMRAD theses 137; logical coherence 150; scope of research 148; signposting 160; voice 163
confidence 32
consistency 150–152
contingency 39, 44
contractions 172
conventions 171–173
correctness, editing for 170
counselling services 66, 189
countdown tickers 34
'creative' work 141–142
critical commentaries 141–142
criticism 94–95, 142, 168
'crunch' stage 9, 20–27, 67, 104

data 34–35
deadlines 67–70, 104; goal setting 29; project plans 44; time budgets 37, 39; tracking your progress 32, 34
decision-making 21, 187–189
'deep work' 122
deletions 152
deliberate practice 60
deliverables 44
Dening, Greg 4
disabilities 75, 89
disciplinary norms 143
discussion 136–137, 144, 151, 163
distractions 41, 124–125

doctoral support staff 188–189
drafts 49, 51; editing 175; first 18–19, 72–73, 77, 113, 116–119, 120, 165; liberated writing 116–117; multiple 114, 115; supervisor policies 91; Thesis Boot Camp 3; writing cycle 113; zero drafts 108, 116–117, 118, 120–121
Dweck, Carol 82–83

editing 34, 49, 77, 174–175; structural 128–160; style 128, 162, 168–171; vocabulary 171–174; writing cycle 112, 113
emails 24, 26
emotions 193
EndNote 171
episteme 180
ergonomics 63–64
errors 99, 114, 147
evidence 14, 18, 169; 'Big Book' theses 138; dealing with supervisors 95, 97; logical progression 146, 147–148
examiners 18, 81, 143, 148–149, 156, 173–174
exegeses 141–142
exercise 64
exhaustion 62
expectations 92, 93, 96, 97, 168
experiential learning 4
expert voice 162, 163–165
explorers 50

fact checking 121, 170
failure 23, 81–84
family responsibilities 86, 88, 187
fear of failure 82
feedback 23–24, 49, 51, 55, 148–149, 174–175; assertive communication 95; co-supervisors 102; expectations 92; perfectionist supervisors 99–100; structural editing 130
finishing 7, 177, 179–180, 183, 189–190, 191–197
first drafts 18–19, 72–73, 77, 113, 116–119, 120, 165
fixed mindset 82–83
flow, editing for 131–133
flow (state of concentration) 122
focus 22, 145, 150
food 64–65
formal breaks 189
formatting 114, 121, 170–171
freedom 116–117
friend-colleague supervisors 100–101
friends and family 189

Gantt charts 33, 34
gaps, editing for 131
Gardiner, Maria 78
generative writing 119–121
genres 136–143
gifts 193–194
Glass, Ira 76, 77
goals: deadlines 67, 68–69; goal setting 28–31, 32; setting your pace 34–35; time budgets 37, 39; tracking your progress 32–33; *see also* targets
graduation 194
grammar 162, 167–168, 170
Grammarly 99, 170
grief 193
Grint, Keith 181
Groopman, Jerome 181
growth mindset 82–83
guilt 68, 195

handwriting 165
harassment 103
headings 154–155, 166–167
headphones 124
Headspace 67
health 59, 62–67, 87, 89, 104
hedging language 148, 152
heuristics 181
holidays 61–62

ideolect 164
Imposter Syndrome 74–75
IMRAD (Introduction, Methods, Results And Discussion) theses 136–137
inclusion, editing for 131
interdisciplinary theses 143, 146, 167, 173–174
intermission from studies 62, 185, 189
international students 86, 88
interruptions 43, 98–99
introductions: 'Big Book' theses 138; bridge sections 132; consistency 151, 152; IMRAD theses 136; logical coherence 150; scope of

research 148; signposting 156–157, 160; voice 163

jargon 172, 173–174
jobs 193, 195, 196–197
jointly written papers 140
JOMA (Just One More Article) Syndrome 78–79, 99
Jones, Denise 125
journals 35–36, 52–54, 188

Kamler, Barbara 57, 107–108, 144
Kara, Helen 196
Kearns, Hugh 78
Kiley, Margaret 81, 143
knowledge 149, 180–181

Lamott, Anne 116
Le Fanu, Sheridan 194
learning: experiential 4; lifelong 180
length of thesis 134–135; *see also* word counts
liberated writing 116–117
lifelong learning 180
limitations 148
linking structures 132–133
literature reviews 144, 148
logical progression 146–150, 169
loss 193

Mason, Shannon 140
measurement 29, 151
meditation 66–67
Mendeley 171
mental health 59, 66–67, 69, 87, 89
Merga, Margaret 140

methodologists 50
methods 136, 141, 144, 148, 163, 172
micromanaging supervisors 97–99
milestones 5, 18, 60, 70, 80, 179
mindfulness 67
mindset 82–83
'mini-maps' 157
mistakes 99, 114, 147
monographs 138, 139
motivation 31–32, 69
Mullins, Gerry 81, 143
Murray, Rowena 196
music 124
myths 59–70, 87

Newport, Cal 122
nonsense words 120
norms 143, 166–167, 175, 193
notes 121
nutrition 64–65

oral defences 196

pace: setting your 34–35
pacemakers 34
Pacheco-Vega, Raul 45
Pang, Alex Soojung-Kim 61
paragraphs 131, 132, 169
passing 23–24, 80–81
passive communication 94
passive voice 167, 172
peer reviewed articles 140
People of Colour 75
perfect sentence vortex 114–116
perfectionism 49, 75–78, 115

perfectionist supervisors 99–100
personal pronouns 165, 166–167, 168, 172
phrase patterning 132–133
phronesis 180–181
physical activity 64
Picoult, Jodi 116
planning 32, 43–45, 92–93, 97, 98, 153
policies 90–91, 134
polishing 112, 114, 121, 162
Pomodoro technique 39–42, 125
'post-show blues' 191–192
posture 63
practical wisdom 181
'practical' work 141–142
procrastination 76, 78, 123
productivity 33, 60–61, 124–125
progress tracking 29, 31–36
project definition 11–19
project management 6–7, 9–10, 28–45; goal setting 28–31; Pomodoro technique 39–42; scheduling 42–43; setting your pace 34–35; time budgets 36–39; tracking your progress 31–36
project plans 43–45, 92–93, 97, 98
proofreading 34
publications 139–141, 151
punctuation 169

qualitative research 137
questions 12–16, 52; answer statement 17–18; consistency 151; first draft 19; structural edit 129; theoretical structure of the whole thesis 144
quitting 7, 183–190
quotations 138, 147, 169, 170

reading 78–79, 121
references 114, 121, 134, 170
refinement 19
reflection 177, 181
relationships 57, 103–104
relaxation 65, 66–67
research: collaborative 195; consistency 150; final projects 149; scope 15; signposting 159; thinking stage 121; working styles 50
Research Degree Insiders 45
research journals 35–36, 52–54, 188
research questions 12–16, 52; answer statement 17–18; consistency 151; first draft 19; structural edit 129; theoretical structure of the whole thesis 144
resources 44
results 136–137
reverse outlines 99, 133, 153–155
rewards 33
rewriting 152
rituals 122–123, 124
rock-star supervisors 101–102
rules 166–167

Salmons, Janet 196
schedules 42–43

scholarly conventions 171–173
scholarly style 162, 166–168
sciences 137, 167, 168
scope 15, 22, 23, 148, 151
Scrivener 34
self-criticism 72–84
self-management 57, 62–67, 87
self-talk 73
sentences: chunking 169; perfect sentence vortex 114–116; topic 132, 150, 154–155
sequence, editing for 130–131
Shut Up and Write (SUAW) groups 125–126
signal words 159–160
signing off 91
signposting 52, 155–160
size limits 134–135; *see also* word counts
sleep 65–66, 89
SMART (Specific, Measurable, Achievable, Relevant, and Timebound) goals 30
software 34, 41, 170, 171
spell checkers 99, 170
spelling 114, 170
sticker method 35
Street, Helen 69
strengths 10, 47–48, 50–52, 53, 55, 188
stress 59–60, 70, 87, 89; breaks 61; deadlines 104; finishing a PhD 193; stress management 66–67; Thesis Boot Camp 3
structural editing 128–160
structuring 113, 118

stuck, feeling 83–84, 86–89, 183
style editing 128, 162, 168–171
style guides 166–167, 171
style, scholarly 162, 166–168
submission 7, 91, 92, 177, 179–180
supervisors 6, 18, 87, 90–104, 107; challenging styles 96–104; communication with 93–95; decision-making support 188; feedback from 23–24, 148–149, 174–175; first drafts 117, 118–119; gifts to 193–194; logical mistakes 147; meeting with 25; rights and responsibilities 90–93
supervisory panels 91
support 87–88, 188–189
Sword, Helen 107, 167
SWOT (Strengths, Weaknesses, Opportunities, and Threats) Analysis 188

targets 3, 34, 67, 70; *see also* goals
'taste gap' 76–77, 118
techne 180
technical language 173–174
technical structure 129
temptations 123–124
theoretical structure of the whole thesis 99, 129, 144–146
theory 148
Thesis Boot Camp (TBC) 2–4, 69, 118, 188
thesis, definition of 12

thesis questions 12–16, 52; answer statement 17–18; consistency 151; first draft 19; structural edit 129; theoretical structure of the whole thesis 144
thesis types 136–143
The Thesis Whisperer 45
thinking 112–113, 121
Thomson, Pat 57, 107–108, 144
time management 33; Pomodoro technique 39–42; project plans 43–45; schedules 42–43; time budgets 22, 36–39, 43, 66
'Tiny Texts' strategy 144, 151
tone 162
topic sentences 132, 150, 154–155
tracking your progress 29, 31–36
types of thesis 136–143

uncertainty 193

vacations 61–62
viva voce 196
vocabulary 162, 171–174
voice 162, 163–165

weaknesses 47–48, 50–51, 188

web-blockers 123
wellbeing 63, 64, 70, 104
'will it pass?' question 23–24
women 75, 94
word counts 29, 34, 36, 134–135, 175
work commitments 88–89
working-class backgrounds 75
working hours 59, 60–61
working styles 47–52
writers block 45
writing 107–108; generative 119–121; getting in the zone 122–125; liberated 116–117; perfect sentence vortex 114–116; as a performance 72–73; Pomodoro technique 40–41; Shut Up and Write groups 125–126; Thesis Boot Camp 3–4; time budgets 22, 36–39; working it out by writing it out 117–119; writing cycle 111–114; *see also* editing
writing journals 35–36

zero drafts 108, 116–117, 118, 120–121
Zotero 171

Taylor & Francis Group
an informa business
Taylor & Francis eBooks
www.taylorfrancis.com
A single destination for eBooks from Taylor & Francis with increased functionality and an improved user experience to meet the needs of our customers.
90,000+ eBooks of award-winning academic content in Humanities, Social Science, Science, Technology, Engineering, and Medical written by a global network of editors and authors.
TAYLOR & FRANCIS EBOOKS OFFERS:
A streamlined experience for our library customers
A single point of discovery for all of our eBook content
Improved search and discovery of content at both book and chapter level
REQUEST A FREE TRIAL
support@taylorfrancis.com
Routledge
Taylor & Francis Group
CRC Press
Taylor & Francis Group

Printed in Great Britain
by Amazon